BIRTHI

AUTHOR: MII

MW01113655

# BIRTHING YOUR PROMISE

Library of Congress cataloging-in-Publication Data:
Gloria A. Blackwell

Note from the Author: The interpretation of some scriptures may not be fully expounded upon; therefore you should search and research the scriptures for yourselves in order to get a clearer understanding.

Unless otherwise noted, all scripture quotations are from the New King James Version of the Bible. Copyright @ 1964, 1966, 1968, by Thomas Nelson, Inc.

1

# BIRTHING YOUR PROMISE

ISBN: 978-0-9748006-2-2

Front cover drawn by: Breana Fisher
Naruinufan14@gmail.com

Graphic Design by Shawna Sheffler
Shawna.Sheffler@gmail.com

Printed in the United States of America

Printed by Imprint Now Printing

To order copies of this book

Contact: Minister Gloria A. Blackwell
P.O Box 1362
Clinton Md. 20735
or
E-mail: Birthingyourpromise@yahoo.com

# Dedication

This book is dedicated in loving memory of My Son Gregory S. Meredith, My Dad Benjamin L. Meredith, and My Grandmother Emma Ware Meredith.

**"SON"**

**"DAD"**

**"GRANDMA"**

"The memory of them will forever live in my heart."

**"MY MOM"**

"To My Mom Hilda Mae Meredith, I Love You and I honor you while you are yet alive."

To My Children Jeffery, Anthony, and Noelle Blackwell: And to all My Grandchildren.

"May all the promises of God be fulfilled in your life."

# BIRTHING YOUR PROMISE

I cannot complete this dedication without acknowledging and honoring my new to the family grandson. I do not know his name. I found out about him a few years ago. I didn't want to believe my son left another son here. I was at my mom's house one day and I was handed a picture of him, and I was asked, who is this? And I answered, is that Greg. Greg is my deceased son. My sister explained that the picture I was holding is a picture of the little boy she told me about a few years ago. This is the picture of him.

I hope to meet him and his mom one day. I was told that she showed up at my mom's house because her son has been asking her questions about his father and his family; and she wanted him to meet them. I prayed that God would make known to me the truth, and I now have my answer. I am now praying that I will meet him in person, him and his mom.

## Acknowledgement

I want to thank God for making all things possible, and for inspiring me to write this book. It is he who made himself known to me, and revealed his word to me; for this I am forever grateful. I give all praise, honor, and glory to God. I am thankful for God for choosing me, and causing me to know and understand that he is God, and there is no other god beside him. I thank God for never giving up on me, and for being faithful to his word.

I also want to acknowledge Breana Fisher for her creativity in creating the cover for this book. She was able to capture the vision that I had in mind, and she wasted no time in putting the vision on paper, Thank You Breana.

I want to thank Lisa Jackson for selling me an ISBN number for my book. I greatly appreciate her support

And last but not least my daughter's godmother Denise Westray. Thank you so much for all of your help and support. Thank you for making this book come together.

# *BIRTHING YOUR PROMISE*

## TABLE OF CONTENTS

# INTRODUCTION

God's promises to man, and for man was establish before the foundation of the world. He strategically settled his word in heaven and then settled it on earth. The book of Revelation is very clear about how the plan of God materialized. The book of Revelation is where we see God's blue print in heaven, and his revelation of what he was making to manifest on earth.

The book of Revelation is the revelation of Jesus Christ. The word "revelation" refers to an unveiling or exposure of God's program for the world through Christ.

God has put his word inside of us. His word is his promise. Every word spoken by God is good. If God words were a check you can cash it without it ever bouncing. There was a time when there were a saying that goes like this - "My word is my bond". This simply means that when a person spoke something; you had that person's word, and their word was supposed to be good. This statement was meant to be taken as true to what was spoken. We are living in a time when people are more desperate than ever. People are looking for answers, and are becoming discouraged because many proclaim to have their answers, only to be disappointed. Your answer is in the Holy Bible which contains the word of God. God's word is true. We need to take God at his word. **Let God be true and every man a liar.**

The book of the Bible contains sixty-six books. It is divided into two parts; the Old and New Testament. The first book is Genesis meaning beginning and the last book is Revelation. Revelation comes from the first word of the book in Greek. That word is "apokalypsis", which means "the unveiling of something previously unrevealed.

When you read and understand the word of God, you are empowered by God to deliver his word when you take ownership of his word and speak it like you believe what God has spoken is true.

**You are God's representative.** If you can go to school, and study it's curriculum, go to work and learn its requirement, join a fraternity or sorority and obey its rituals by doing what that organization tell you to do; then how come you seem to have a problem doing what God instruct you to do. It seems to me that we have become a people who honor's a man's word above God's word. We are the vessels of God, made by God to carry and deliver his word.

God's word is like a fruitful womb of a woman, it keeps on producing and reproducing. As a child cannot return to its mother's womb; neither can God's word return unto him. God's word will perform into the thing where into he sends it. God made us to be victorious, and to have the victory in every situation and circumstances. He has placed everything we need on the inside of us. It is our duty to search the scriptures daily and meditate on the word day and night, then will God make our way prosperous.

My hope is that this book will bring clarity to your understanding; ignite the furnace of your spirit, and to empower you to speak with authority, and boldness according to God's promises.

My hope is for you to come to know without a doubt that the devil is already defeated, and to live victoriously like he really is. Satan was defeated in heaven, and on earth. Once Satin was defeated in heaven; he fell from his glory, and God sent his son (the word) Jesus to defeat Satan on earth too. The only power Satan have over you is the power you give over to him. Jesus openly made a show of the devil and took back everything the devil stole from us, and reconciled us back to God.

**Jesus blotted out the handwriting of ordinances that was against us, which was contrary**

to us, and took it out of the way, nailing it to his cross; and having spoiled principalities, and powers he made a show of them openly, triumphing over them in it. (Colossians 2:14)

It was Jesus who came and rescued us from our enemies. He did it so that we may serve him without fear, and without being in bondage.

Blessed be the Lord God of Israel; for he hath visited and redeemed his people. And hath raised up an horn of salvation for us in the house of his servant David. As he spoke by the mouth of his holy prophets, which have been since the world began: That we should be saved from our enemies, and from the hand of all that hate us; To perform the mercy promised to our fathers, and to remember his holy covenant: That he would grant unto us, that we being delivered out of the hand of our enemies might serve him without fear. (Luke 1:68-74)

If you confess that you are a believer, here is your one chance to believe what God has spoken. Your mission and your assignment here on earth are to carry out the will and plan of God; and to witness that he is. His plan for you is to triumph over the enemy.

He has given you everything you need to win. God's desire is for you to hearken unto his word, and to do what he hath instructed you to do. God's plan for you is an unfailing plan **that will work if you work it**. Your participation is vital. God has done all of the work for you, all you have to do is to go where he tells you to go, and do what he tells you to do.

Your physical body is only made of dust; which will return to the ground, but you were created in three parts, body, soul and spirit. Your spirit is eternal. Do not let your flesh keep you from giving birth to your promise. You have the ability to operate in the same power that Jesus demonstrated. If Jesus thought it not robbery to be equal with God, then you shouldn't either. **Jesus said that he and his Father are one.** We as God's children should take on this same mind set of Jesus, and be one (in agreement) with God. **Jesus said, He does what he hears the Father says and doeth it.**

It is God who created us, formed us, and breathed the breath of life in us. He placed inside of us this treasure (his word) inside of our earthly body called a vessel. We are uniquely and wonderfully made by the potter (Creator God) who formed us with his hands; he started with a lump of clay (dust of the earth) and water (his spirit). He then began to shape the clay into a form as the table top (the world) spins: While the clay is forming and shaping in the Master's hands, sometimes it becomes marred even while it is in the hand of the potter. But, the potter is able to make you again another. He has the power to shape you and reshape you.

God's word is able to keep you, shape you and

reshape you again. God assures us in his word when he spoke to his Prophet Jeremiah saying, **Arise and go down to the potter's house, and there I will cause thee to hear my words. Then I went down to the potter's house, and, he wrought a work on the wheels. And the vessel that he made of clay was marred in the hand of the potter: so he made it again another vessel, as seemed good to the potter to make it. Then the word of the Lord came to me, saying, O house of Israel, cannot I do with you as this potter? Saith the Lord. Behold, as the clay is in the potter's hand, so are ye in mine hand, O house of Israel. (Jeremiah 18:1-6)**

We all at some point in life have been victimized, and criticized by someone. In some cases we've been used, misused, abused and mishandled by those who were entrusted to us. We all can testify to being in a disfigured mess, and will probably still be in the mess if it had not been God who is known to be the Potter, who was able to put us back together again.

There are some of us who do not know the mercy of God and is living life in a disfigured state because they don't know who they are, and who God is. The psalmist said it best when she said, **"The Potter wants to put you back together again"**. God is not a God who has to be proven, He has already proven himself; there will be nothing else. Don't be like the Pharisees and Sadducees who both were looking for a sign. Because even when the signs were seen-they still did not believe. "You either believe God or you don't".

This book is written to those of you who knows, and understand that the kingdom of God is within them; my hope is to stir up the gift within you, and to provoke you to visit, and revisit the word of God which will empower you to triumph over all your enemies.

My prayer is that the spirit filled words written on these pages of this book will cause your baby to leap in your womb, and that your faith will become stronger.

And for those of you who will read this book and do not know that the kingdom of God is within you, I pray that the eyes of your understanding will be enlighten; and the spirit filled words written on these pages will be like sperm, and your spirit be like a woman ovulating so that when your spirit receive it, it will cause conception.

I pray by the Spirit of the Living God that you will receive the promise of God which is freely given to you by faith.

# THE BEGINNING

In the beginning God created the heaven and the earth. He created and furnished the heaven before establishing creation on the earth. The earth is described as being without form, and void; and darkness was upon the face of the deep. The reason for the darkness was because God have not yet spoken in the atmosphere of the earth. He was establishing the creation in heaven to make preparation for his chosen people on earth. Before furnishing the earth God created and furnished the heaven. He created the angels and the entire heavenly host. He named them, and gave them free will and power.

The reason I say that the angels had free will is because how else would Lucifer decide to transgress against the almighty God. Lucifer was fashioned like no other angel. His name in Latin means morning star, and in Hebrew it means bright one. God gave him great powers, but not all power. I believe the beginning of

# THE BEGINNING

God's plan for earth began in the book of **(Revelation Chapter 12)**. The Apostle John began his writing in the book of **(Revelation 1:1)** by saying, **The Revelation of Jesus Christ, which God gave unto his servant's things which must shortly come to pass.**

My first encounter with this book and this particular chapter was in 1997, when I was a member at Galilee Baptist Church in Suitland Md., where the honorable Pastor Eugene Weathers was the pastor. I was enrolled in the Elijah academy for ministers in training. One of my assignments was to read the book of **Revelation** and interpret what it meant. When I reached the **12th chapter** of the book of **Revelation**, It stopped me in my track.

I wanted to know who was this woman and what was she doing in heaven? She wasn't an angel, because angels are neither male nor female. I believe that she was in the mind of God and that he began to draw a picture of this woman as he envisioned her to be. I believe that he then began speaking what he internalize, and his vision became what he said. The God of all creation sketched out his plan as a blue print of what he had in mind, and I believe that the devil got a peak of God's creation and over heard what God had spoken; and he then became jealous. After all, God's creation of a woman was more beautiful than Lucifer. The garment that the woman wore gave off a radiant of God's Glory, adorn as his bride; surely, this had cause jealousy to come up in Lucifer's heart. She was carrying within her what would someday rule over him.

The Bible gives a description of Lucifer (the devil) as an angel of light, perfect in beauty, and every precious stone was his covering; the Sardis, the topaz, the diamond, the beryl, the onyx, the jasper, the sapphire, the emerald, the carbuncle, and the gold. It's no wonder why he would look upon the beauty of this woman and hate the fact that she was created more beautiful than all his covering.

This woman is the most unspoken of woman in the Bible. This woman was definitely like no other woman that I have ever read about in our bible stories. Therefore, it sparked a curiousness inside of me that caused me to question who she was. Not only that, I wanted to know who this baby was.

While attending Galilee Baptist church a girlfriend of mine name Shona Fields was also and in training to become a license ordained minister. When I was doing my reading, and research, I asked her about the text. She said to me that the baby is Jesus. Not that Jesus was born, because he was not. She explained to me that it was just a metaphor. What I mean by a metaphor is that a metaphor is a word or symbol used in the place of something else.

# THE BEGINNING

This is not to confuse anyone who Jesus Christ is; the bible clearly states in **(John 1:1)** that **"In the beginning was the word (Jesus) and the word was with God and the word was God"**. What I wanted to point out in this particular text is not the fact that the child was born in heaven, but the woman who was spoken of in heaven. And nobody that I know of had ever mention or preached concerning this woman. If they have, I don't recall anyone speaking in regard to this woman. It could be because the woman is a metaphor for the church (the bride of Christ). What I can say is this; that God knew what was in Satan's heart when he created him, and he knew that he would need to launch a plan that will annihilate the works of the enemy from the beginning of time. God describes Satan before his fall in **(Ezekiel 28:15), Thou (Satan) wast perfect in thy ways from the day that thou wast created, till iniquity was found in thee.** I believe since God knew the end from the beginning, he prepared a plan that will defeat the devil.

This woman was created beautiful, and she represented Israel God's chosen people. She was a woman clothed with the sun and the moon under her feet. This too is a metaphor that represented power that alludes to God's promise of dominion. And upon her head is a crown of twelve stars that relates to the twelve tribes of Israel, and a picture of royalty.

# THE BEGINNING

This woman is the mother of all women, in her original state; she represents us all. It is here in the twelfth chapter of the book of Revelation that God allow us to peak into heaven and to reveal to us how it all began. I can imagine God drawing and painting a picture of the woman he had in mind, and being the artist that he is; I imagine that his drawing had life to it, sought of like the animated Disney characters created by Mr. Walt Disney. The reason I used Mr. Disney is to give you an idea of how creative God is himself, and he made us to be a creator just like him.

God had in mind all the time for a woman to give birth to a male child (his word) that will deliver us, redeem us, regenerate us, and reconcile us back to him. Let us look into the mind of God through scriptures, and look into heaven, where it all began.

## (REVELATION 12:1-17)

**And there was a wonder in heaven: a woman clothed with the Sun, and the moon under her feet, and upon her head a crown of twelve stars: And she being with child cried travailing in birth, and pained to be delivered.**

**And there appeared another wonder in heaven; and behold a great red dragon, having seven heads and ten horns and seven crowns upon his heads, and**

his tail drew the third part of the stars of heaven, and did cast them to the earth: And the dragon stood before the woman which was ready to be delivered, for to devour her child as soon as it was born.

And she brought forth a man child. Who was to rule all nations with a rod of iron: and her child was caught up unto God, and to his throne. And the woman fled into the wilderness, where she hath a place prepared of God; that they should feed her there a thousand two hundred and threescore days.

And there was war in heaven: Michael and his angels fought against the dragon; and the dragon fought and his angels, and prevailed not; neither was their place found any more in heaven. And the great dragon was cast out, that old serpent, called the Devil, and Satan, which deceiveth the whole world; he was cast out into the earth, and his angels were cast out with him.

And I heard a loud voice saying in heaven, now is come salvation, and strength, and the kingdom of our God, and the power of his Christ; for the accuser of our brethren is cast down, which accused them before our God day and night. And they overcame him by the blood of the lamb and by the word of their testimony; and they loved not their lives unto death.

# THE BEGINNING

**Therefore rejoice ye heavens, and ye that dwell in them. Woe to the inhabiters of the earth and of the sea! For the devil is come down unto you, having great wrath, because he knoweth that he hath but a short time. And when the dragon saw that he was cast unto the earth, he persecuted the woman which brought forth the man child.**

As we can see from reading this scripture, there were two great wonders in heaven. The first was a woman and the second was a great red dragon. These two are the main characters.

This story in heaven reveals to us the plan of God for us on earth. I pray for your understanding to be enlightened, and that your spiritual eyes will be open. God knew the plan that he had in mind for us, a plan to send his word in the earth. He knew that Satan would attempt to interfere, and try to stop his plan and the purpose of man.

God created man in his image, and he fashioned him in his likeness (a speaking spirit and a creator). He then equipped man with everything he would need to be victorious on earth. He made man another speaking spirit like himself. But, sad to say men have not yet discovered the power of his own words, or should I say, He has not taken advantage of the weapon entrusted to him.

# THE BEGINNING

My brothers and sisters my wish is for you to understand that this fight you are in- has already been won. What I would like for you to understand is that the war that we are in right now-started in heaven, ended in heaven, and picked up again on earth. Just like Satan was defeated in heaven it is God's will and purpose for him to be defeated here on earth too; which we will see later in the story. I am inclined to believe that the fight is over words. The question is, whose word will you believe? Words rule and words are the most powerful weapon there is. "Will you believe God's word or will you believe the Devil's word"?

**The word of God upholds all things by the words of his power.    (Hebrew 1:3)**

Let me make this clear to you readers, the devil fell from heaven. When he fell; he fell into God's unfinished creation. God had not yet spoken on earth for things to appear on earth as of yet. God then came down from heaven and started speaking into a dark and empty world. If you choose to believe the devil over God you too are in danger of falling just like the devil. The question is asked, whose report will you believe? The apostle Paul made it plain and clear about the fight we are in; in the book of **(Ephesians 6:12) – For we wrestle not against flesh and blood, but against principalities, against powers, against the rulers of darkness of this world, against spiritual wickedness**

**in high places.** The Devil is the god of this world who opposes God's word.

When the devil was in heaven he stirred up strife and division among the angels first. He became full of pride. In **(Isaiah 14:13)** it says, **For thou (Satan) said in thine heart, I will exalt my throne above the stars of God; I will sit also upon the mount of the congregation, in the sides of the north. I will ascend above the heights of the clouds; I will be like the most high.** He wanted to be like God, but His rebellion against God stripped him of God's glory.

If we were to pay attention to the character of Satan; we can see how man has taken on that character in the fall. This one particular characteristic is pride. **Pride comes before a fall.** We can learn a vital lesson from our enemy because Satan used this same strategy against Eve in the garden.

**(Genesis 3:4-5), And the serpent said unto the woman, Ye shall not surely die; for God doth know that in the day ye eat there of, then your eyes shall be opened, and ye shall be as gods, knowing good and evil.** Satan planted a thought in Eve's mind by suggesting something to her which she had already possess. She was already like God. **(Genesis 1:27) says, So God created man in his own image, in the image of God created he him; male and female created he them.**

# THE BEGINNING

When the woman Eve ate of the tree her eyes were open to the natural things of her surroundings. She is now experiencing something she never experienced before. Her disobedience awakened a fleshly appetite. When God created man upon the earth he created him as a triune being like himself. He created man spirit, soul and body. After the woman ate of the fruit she then turns to her husband to offer him some of the fruit that she had just eaten. I can imagine her telling him how good the fruit taste and how good it makes one feel. He then listens to his wife and partake of the forbidden fruit that God instructed them not to eat from. The two of them are now aware of their physical appearance. **(Genesis 3:7) – And the eyes of them both were opened, and they knew that they were naked; and they sewed leaves together, and made themselves aprons.** They both have lost their spiritual sight.

The reason I say this is because their attitude had change. In the beginning the woman was bold, and courageous to stand up to Satan. And now she has become afraid, fearful, shameful, and forgetful. Once they discovered that they were naked; they both felt ashamed. They forgot what God sounded like after they listened to the voice of the devil **(note:** sin will deafen your spiritual hearing). After the man and woman disobeyed God the two of them hid themselves from the one who created them.

# THE BEGINNING

**And they heard the voice of the Lord God walking in the garden in the cool of the day; and Adam and his wife hid themselves from the presence of the Lord God amongst the trees of the garden. (Genesis 3:8)**

If we were to look at today's day and time we will find people doing the same thing. You have people running away from God instead of running to God. How many times have you heard for yourself a believer who has sinned against God; and they too become ashamed to admit their fault so they run by staying away from church. How about those who make excuses about why they don't go to church? This happens all the time. People have the tendency to run away from God instead of running to God. The devil wants to keep you out of fellowship with God. Because he knows that God will receive you as his own. The devil also know that God will forgive you and take you back and love you as if you had never sinned. It is the devil who accuses you and reminds you of your sin, **"Not God"**.

This is not to say that you need to be in church to be save; But save people goes to church. **(Hebrews 10:25) - Not forsaking the assembling of ourselves together, as the manner of some is; but exhorting one another: and so much the more, as you see the day approaching.**

# THE BEGINNING

Let's look back to our foundational text in **(Revelation 12)**.

**And there appeared a great wonder in heaven; a woman clothed with the sun and the moon under her feet and upon her head a crown of twelve stars: And she being (pregnant) with child, cried, and travailing in birth pain ready to deliver. (Revelation 12:1-2)**

This woman in heaven gave birth to our savior in heaven who will rule over and defeat the enemy. He was birth to save us from the evil one, and from all of Satan's works. The bible said that the baby was caught up to God as soon as it was born; this is to indicate Christ ascension.

I want to make something clear to you all, those of you who are reading this book to remember **this one** thing; Satan came to kill, steal, and destroy. Jesus came so that we may have life and have it more abundantly. When Satan saw that the woman was about to give birth, he stood before her to devour her child as soon as it was born. Please understand that the birthing of this child is a metaphor of God's word going forth in the earth. The revelation of this text is the revealing of the mystery. He that has an ear let him hear what the spirit is saying to the church.

When the child was born he was caught up to God; after the devil slain the child. **How do I know this? I know this because the lamb was slain before the foundation of the world. Therefore the baby was slain just before being caught up to God. (Revelation: 5:6-10)**

**And I beheld, and, lo, in the midst of the throne and of the four beast, and in the midst of the elders, stood a lamb as it had been slain, having seven horns and seven eyes which are the seven Spirits of God sent forth into all the earth.**

**And he came and took the book out of the right hand of him that sat upon the throne,**

**And when he had taken the book, the four beasts and four and twenty elders fell down before the Lamb, having every one of them harps, and golden vials full of odors, which are the prayers of the saints.**

**And they sung a new song saying, Thou art worthy to take the book, and to open the seals thereof: for thou wast slain, and hast redeemed us to God by thy blood out of every kindred, and tongue, and people, and nation;**

**And hast made us unto our God kings and**

priest; and we shall reign on earth.

**Verse 12 - Worthy is the Lamb that was slain to receive power, and riches and wisdom, and strength, and honor, and glory, and blessing.**

**(Revelation 13:8) says, And all that dwell upon the earth shall worship him, whose names are not written in the book of life of the Lamb slain from the foundation of the world.** This is where the teaching comes from that we were saved from the foundation of the world. The sacrifice was made for our sins before the earth was furnished. God has pre-destined us to win and to have victory over the devil from the foundation of the world. We are winners by what God has already done. He simply wants us to obey his word so that we can have all the blessings that he promise we could have. Satan is a liar. He is described as the father of lies. He is known to be a thief and a murderer. He is also known to oppose the word of God, and he has opposed it from the beginning. Your challenge is to take hold of God's word and to keep it, no matter what you hear, see, feel, or understand. **"IF GOD SAID IT THEN THAT SETTLES IT".**

**Trust in the Lord with all thine heart; and lean not unto thine own understanding. In all thy ways acknowledge him, and he shall direct thy paths. (Proverbs 3:5-6)**

**Submit yourselves therefore to God. Resist the devil, and he will flee from you. (James 4:7)**

When Jesus was here on earth he had to resist the devil time after time. Whenever the devil tempted Jesus He tempted him with the same enticement he used on Eve. Jesus responded simply by reminding Satan of what was written. It is important to know what God's word says in the Bible. This will be your ammunition. The devil only wins when you give in to his suggestions. If you stand firm to your confession by saying what God says and not surrender to the enemy, you will win every time. Even if it hurts, even if it looks like Satan is winning, stand fast to your confessions.

**For I reckon that the sufferings of this present time are not worthy to be compared with the glory which shall be revealed in us. (Romans 8:18)**

When Jesus was here on earth, he suffered many things. He was talked about, he was tempted, he was lied on, spit on, and hit on. Jesus said, if they hated him, the world will hate you too. But, he also said, be of good cheer (courage) I (Jesus) has already overcome the world.

**And it came to past, after the woman gave birth to the man child, she fled into the wilderness. Where she hath a place prepared of God; that she**

**would be fed for three thousand two hundred and thirty days. (Revelation 12:6)**

This is a very interesting story. The story now moves from heaven to earth.

While the woman was hidden in this prepared place, a war broke out in heaven. **Michael and his angels fought against the dragon (Satan); and his angels. And they prevailed not; neither was there any place found any more in heaven. And the great dragon was cast out, that old serpent, called the Devil, and Satan, which deceiveth the whole world: he was cast out into the earth, and his angels were cast out with him. And when the dragon saw that he was cast unto the earth he persecuted the woman which brought forth the man child. (Revelation 12:13)**

What a story! A war broke out in heaven first, and now that the devil is here on earth he have been causing wars and rumors of wars. The dragon (Devil) was cast out of heaven unto the earth, and he continued what he started in heaven by persecuting the woman. He has great wrath against us especially women. He has persecuted the women here on earth by hurting and destroying the men, the children, and the family. Remember how the woman in heaven gave birth to a male child. And that male child was going to rule over Satan. The devil wanted to prevent the woman from giving birth to our savior, and our deliverer, but God's plan trumped the devils plan. This revelation should empower you and encourage you to never, ever give up. God made us to win. The devil fights us by frustrating our human nature and the natural things we possess. The material things are temporal; they can be seen and replaced. **(2 Corinthians 10:3-5) says, For though we walk in the flesh, we do not war (fight) after the flesh; (For the weapons of our warfare are not carnal, but mighty through God for pulling down of strongholds;) Casting down imaginations, and every high thing that exalteth itself against the knowledge of God, and bringing into captivity every thought to the obedience of Christ.**

The Lord God himself chose us (humans). He thought more about us than he did his angels. He put his word (Son) in us that even the angels inquire of God concerning this.

**What is man, that thou art mindful of him? And the son of man, that thou visitest him? For thou hast made him a little lower than the angels, and hast crowned him with glory and honor. Thou madest him to have dominion over the works of thy hands; thou hast put all things under his feet. (Psalm 8:4-6)**

# THE BEGINNING

The devil envied, and coveted the glory of God that was placed on man- kind; after all the glory of God was once upon him. I am not writing this book to cause any more division among us than it already is. But I am writing this book in hope to enlighten your understanding as God's chosen people. God created a woman in heaven with the thought in mind to put his word inside of man-kind as it is in himself. What I do personally believe is that God created a woman because he is a God of purpose. When God created male and female he created them both in his image. He also created male and female for the purpose of reproduction.

**Note:** A male and another male cannot reproduce together; neither can a female and another female reproduce together. A human and an animal cannot reproduce together. God made everything to reproduce after its kind.

The creator God made humans so much like himself that whatever they needed he has already placed inside of them. For example a man does not have a womb but he has seed within him to deposit into a womb to cause reproduction; and a woman has eggs inside of her womb which cannot be produced without the deposit of a male seed. With this being said, God is a seed giver and everything that he had deposited his seeds into produces, and bares fruit after its kind.

# THE BEGINNING

I love the way God thinks because he creates everything with purpose. It's not that women are more superior then a man because of a womb, nor because of the church which is the bride of Christ is modeled as a woman, No I am not saying that at all. God is a God of purpose. When God created everything he created it to produce and reproduce after its kind. He did it in such a way that he would not have to do it again.

**And God said, Let the earth bring forth grass, the herb yielding seed, and the fruit tree yielding fruit after his kind, whose seed is in itself, upon the earth: and it was so. (Genesis 1:1)**

**(Verses 20, 21, 22)**

**And God said, Let the waters bring forth abundantly the moving creature that hath life, and fowl that may fly above the earth in the open firmament of heaven.**

**And God created great whales, end every living creature that moveth, which the waters brought forth abundantly, after their kind: and God saw that it was good.**

**And God blessed them, saying, Be fruitful, and multiply, and fill the waters in the seas, and let fowl multiply in the earth.**

**(Verses 24, 25)**

## THE BEGINNING

**And God said, Let the earth bring forth the living creature after his kind, cattle, and creeping thing, and beast of the earth after his kind: and it was so.**

**And God made the beast of the earth after his kind, and cattle after their kind, and every thing that creepeth upon the earth after his kind: and God saw that it was good.**

God continued to speak all creation into existence until he made man. Understand that man could not reproduce another human until God created his wife. Let me first say that God is a God of order. God's infinite mind saw his church (his bride), and he knew that his bride will need a husband, a help meet, a provider, a covering, and a protector like himself. Therefore in order of the making of male and female God created man and then pulled woman out of man just like he pulled the church (woman) out of himself in heaven, where he created her. I know I have some haters after me for that statement. Some men do not know how important women are to God. Women are so important to God that he instructed men to love their wives as Christ love the church. God compared a woman with being his bride (his church). Listen up women this should speak life and hope to your insecurity. God's love for you is worth more than a man's affirmation.

# THE BEGINNING

**In the beginning was the word, and the word was with God, and the word was God. The same was in the beginning with God. All things were made by him; and without him was not anything made that was made. (John 1:1-3)**

God wrapped himself in human flesh and dwelt among us, and we beheld his glory. We can still have the privilege of beholding his glory by allowing his word to be fruitful in us, and to walk worthy in his presence. I now understand why Jesus had such great compassion for women. He witnessed firsthand the pain and suffering she endured doing her child bearing and birthing in heaven. He also knew that the devil was the one who caused her so much the sorrow. He saw how the devil persecuted her in heaven, and how the devil stood against her as she gave birth. Jesus he understands more than anyone why the devil persecutes the woman like he does.

There was another thing that was revealed to me concerning this woman. The Bible said that she was giving birth to a man child. This man child would be the first created man on earth. God was sending his son, his first born son to become sin for us. I am saying this to say, "As it is in heaven, so shall it be on earth". The creator God of the universe is a God of order. He created man first because of his plan and purpose for man to rule, rein, and to have dominion.

Blessed be God who loves us so much to give us such a great inheritance.

Again I am not trying to be bias concerning gender, by no means; I am not bias here. Women you should understand that you are clothed with God's glory, and it is the devil's job to strip it off of you. He's after your witness, your testimony, and Evangelizing. And to you men, the devil is after your ruler-ship, and authority. He knows if he can get the headship, he then can destroy the family. I know I am offending some people by making this statement, but somebody needs to tell the truth. God created a woman in the beauty of his church, and the man to love and care for his bride.

For years we have been competing with the battle of the sexes. If the truth be told the battle should not be against each other. We are on the same team. We are one body of Jesus Christ, and we need to join forces and fight the good fight of faith together. We have a devil to fight; not each other. God placed his word on the inside of us all. It is the devil's job to infiltrate the word of God by offering his words.

There are some men who like to say that because they were created first they are above women. That is not so, God created man first because God is a God of order and purpose. God pulled the woman from the man's side; and the two became one flesh. Marriage is a partnership. God wanted man to love, lead and cover his wife as Christ love and leads, and cover the church. **Wives, submit yourselves unto your own husbands, as unto the Lord. For the husband is the head of the wife, even as Christ is the head of the church; and he is the savior of the body.**

**Therefore as the church is subject unto Christ, so let the wives be to their own husbands in everything.Husbands love your wives, even as Christ also loved the church, and gave himself for it. (Ephesians 5:22-25)**

The woman was chosen to be a very valuable asset created by God. She was entrusted to carry the word (Son) of God. The devil witnessed the creation of her in heaven and waited for the opportune time to confront her on earth. He heard what God instructed Adam, and what Adam instructed Eve. His job now was to cause her to doubt what God had said to her husband, that's right her husband. God commanded Adam not Eve. This is why God called out to Adam and inquired to Adam what he had done.

The devil thought that he could prevent God's word from coming fourth. He was after the seed (the man child that would be born, that would bruise his head). That seed I am referring to was God's only begotten son who would be born of a woman.

Ladies please understand this, "You are pregnant with promise". This devil is so ignorant because he cannot prevent, stop, or destroy the seed of God. God's seed is incorruptible, and infallible.

God is God. He is life, and he created all things, even the devil. Everything God made he made with the assurance that if it died it will live again. How do I know this because in him is life. His word is eternal.

We have eternal life. **Verily, verily, I say unto you, except a corn of wheat fall into the ground and die, it abideth alone; but if it dies, it bringeth forth much fruit. (John 12:24)**

**Being born again, not of corruptible seed, but of incorruptible seed, by the word of God, which liveth and abideth forever. (1 Peter 1:23)**

When Satan withstood against the woman in heaven, and murdered the baby as soon as it was born; God received the baby to himself, and made him live again. The revelation of this story reveals that God had already pre-plan our deliverance before the beginning of time. Remember now; the baby represents Jesus Christ ascension, after his death burial and resurrection.

A woman is the most valuable and much needed creation out of all of God's creation. I believe she was destined to bring fourth the very thing that is most precious to God, and that is his word. The devil hates God and he hates God's word. Why? Why does he hate God's words? **"Because he is a Hater".** The bible says that iniquity was found in him. The word iniquity means; gross injustice; wickedness, and a violation of right or duty; wicked act or sin.

On the other hand God is Justice, God is Holy, God is Love, God is Joy, God is Peace, God is Patience, God is Kind, God is Longsuffering, God is Truth, God is a Comforter, God is a Husband, a Father, God is the many breasted one, God is light with no darkness in him, God is a savior, a deliverer, God is a road map for life, and he is everything the devil wish he could be. I can go on and on about my God. When the devil speaks; he speaks death, condemnation, lies, slander, and hateful words. The devil is called the Father of lies because he lied from the beginning. There is no truth in him. God's word is life, God's word heals, God's word saves, God's word delivers, his word raises the dead, and his word is all powerful.

Now with that being said, let's look at the devil. The devil words kill (deceive), steal, and destroy. The devil's plan was to get to the woman so that he could destroy all human population. All of generation was in her. He got the woman to eat (disobey God), and now the woman is under the influence of the devil. The woman took the bait and she now believes that what she tasted is good. She then offers the fruit to her husband and He also ate of the fruit.

This is a good example of how things get started. You know how you try something for the first time and you like it? And now you want to tell everybody else about it, because it's soooo... good. Take for instant good food, good drugs, good alcohol, a good movie, a good church, and etc. One person tries it for the first time; like it, and now wants everybody to try it too. The problem is, once you taste something and you like it; it's hard to dislike it.

After Adam and Eve ate from the tree and conceived their children; every child born on earth has taken on the spirit of a disobedient character of both parents that were inherited from their fallen state. This explains how sin entered into the world, and how we all became sinners.

**Wherefore, as by one man sin entered into the world, and death by sin; and so death passed upon all men, for that all have sinned. (Romans 5:12)**

Every one of us has a part of God, and a part of the devil abiding on the inside of us. We have two natures warring on the inside of us. There is an ongoing battle between the two.

**I find then a law, that, when I would do good, evil is present with me.**

**For I delight in the law of God after the inward man: But I see another law in my in my members, warring against the law of my mind, and bringing me into captivity to the law of sin which is in my members.**

**O wretched man that I am! Who shall deliver me from the body of this death?**

**I thank God through Jesus Christ our Lord. So then with the mind I myself serve the law of God: but with the flesh the law of sin. (Romans 7:21-25)**

**But, we have this treasure in earthen vessels, that the excellency of the power may be of God, and not of us. (2 Corinthians 4:7)**

We were not created with the two natures. Because of Adam and Eve's disobedience in the garden we inherited their sin nature. Another problem that exists is that some of us has rejected God's word, and has accepted the lies of the devil. Whenever a person stop listening to God, they open themselves up to hear the lies of the devil, and once they listen to the devil their ears become deaf to hear God, and they too like Eve forget what God had spoken. Then comes the devil to takes advantage of this opportunity by blinding their minds. **(2 Corinthians 4:4) says, In whom the god**

**of this world hath blinded the minds of them which believe not, lest the light of the glorious gospel of Christ, who is the image of God, should shine unto them.**

Don't lose heart my brothers and sisters; be strong by staying in God's word. God has blessed us with all spiritual blessings. We can take no credit for our gifts, and talents, it is the gift of God that works in us, and through us. To God be the glory; for what he is doing, and what he has done. He has given us the victory. Yes, I know someone is asking the question; well why do it look like the enemy is winning? The enemy is not winning, if you are looking at what you can see, you are looking at the wrong thing. Everything that is seen with the natural eye is temporal, and it is subject to change. The natural things is made up to look a certain way, and the enemy will make sure he convince you to believe you are losing, by keeping you looking at the scene (what you can see with your natural eye), instead of the unseen ( what you can't see). God is a Spirit and they that worship him must worship him in spirit and in truth.

**While we look not at the things which are seen, but at the things which are not seen: for the things which are seen are temporal; but the things which are not seen are eternal. (2 Corinthians 4: 18)**

## THE BEGINNING

God has equipped us with everything we need to live victoriously. **According to his divine power hath given unto us all things that pertain unto life, and godliness through the knowledge of him that hath called us to glory and virtue; (1 Corinthians 1:3)**

**And to the woman were given two wings of a great eagle, that she might fly into the wilderness, into her place, where she is nourished for a time, and times, and half a time, from the face of the serpent. And the serpent cast out of his mouth water as a flood after the woman, that he might cause her to be carried away of the flood. (Revelation 12:14-15).**

"Women", you have great strength. The scripture says that God gave the woman two wings of a great eagle. I have researched the meaning of the eagle's wings, and what I discovered was that God has given us divine strength. The eagle represents spiritual protection. When I read this; these two scriptures came to my mind.

**But they that wait upon the Lord shall renew their strength; they shall mount up with wings as eagles; they shall run, and not be weary; they shall walk, and not faint. (Isaiah40:31)**

**He that dwelleth in the secret place of the most high shall abide under the shadow of the almighty.**

# THE BEGINNING

**He shall cover thee with his feathers, and under his wings shalt thou trust: his truth shall be thy shield and buckler.   (Psalm 91:1,4)**

The story now moves from heaven to earth. **And the earth helped the woman, and the earth opened her mouth, and swallowed up the flood which the dragon cast out of his mouth.   (Revelation 12:16)**

Here is where it gets very interesting. Satan who was whipped, beaten, and defeated in heaven is now on planet earth. And the bible says that he has great wrath toward us.

I have heard that Satan took a third of the angels with him. But in **(Revelation 12:4) reads, And his tail ( the great red dragon, Satan) drew the third part of the stars of heaven, and did cast them to the earth.** Satan is so selfish that he was not going down by himself. As he was falling, he took his tail to pull some angels with him. You know this is where we inherited the crabs in the barrel mentality. When Satan was cast out of heaven, he wasn't leaving alone. Have you ever heard someone say, "I am not going out by myself"? Well, there you have it. Satan did not leave heaven alone, and he did not want to go to hell alone either. Scriptures tells us that hell was created for Satan and his angels, but hell enlarged itself, because Satan has influence the mind of the people. And those who reject

Jesus and follow Satan will go to hell with him.

**Therefore hell hath enlarged herself, and opened her mouth without measure; and their glory, and their multitude, and their pomp, and he that rejoiceth, shall descend unto it. (Isaiah 5:14)**

Satan was cast out into the earth, into outer darkness. Earth was a place described as being dark and without form. Listen, If God had not come down and spoke light, we would have been in a state of eternal darkness.

**"And God said, Let there be light".** (Genesis 1:3)

It was as if there was a show down between God and Satan. I mean God really showed the devil; that God is God of heaven and earth. Oh Yes he is!

God started speaking and causing things to be, that was not. After everything was in place; **God said, Let us make man in our image. God formed man from the dust of the ground, male and female created he them. And God Blessed them, and God said unto them, Be fruitful, and multiply, and replenish the earth, and subdue it: and have dominion over the fish of the sea, and over every living thing that moveth upon the earth. (Genesis 1:27-28)**

# THE BEGINNING

I don't know if you get this or not, but your heavenly Father just said that he has **Blessed you, and gave you dominion**. Do you know what that mean? Subdue means to conquer, and to bring under the dominion of another; to bring under control by physical force. This is for all you passive Christians out there, who think that things will happen without you putting forth effort. Stop being soft, and gentle, and take what God said you have, and not what the world say you can have. **He (God) said he has given you dominion**. The question is, when are you going to walk in it? God also said that we are made in his image. We look just like God. It is no wonder why the devil hates us. We have what he use to have, and he is no longer able to possess it. God loves us so much. God loves you and he loves me too. He loves every one of us. His arms are open wide to us all. He is there for whosoever will choose him.

It is time to stop believing the lies of the devil and start believing God. Some of us need to stop believing some of the lies of false prophets and so called pastors who are in positions and feeding you lies. Don't you know that Satan deceives the whole world. No man is exempt. This is not to put the men and women of God who are in leadership positions down. I am simply saying that you need to be careful who you listen to and who you sit under. It is a known fact that what you hear and see can and will influence your spirit.

I also suggest that you make the Lord himself your shepherd, not the pastor who is in pastoral position to lead the sheep, especially if he is not chosen of God and possess having a heart after God's own heart. Search the scriptures daily, and respect those in leadership positions but depend totally on God for guidance.

**I the good shepherd: The good shepherd giveth his life for the sheep: But he that is a hireling, and not the shepherd, whose own the sheep are not, seeth the wolf coming, and leaveth the sheep, and fleeth: And the wolf catcheth them, and scattereth the sheep. The hireling fleeth, because he is a hireling, and careth not for the sheep. I am the good shepherd, and know my sheep, and am known of mine. As the Father knoweth me even so know I the Father; and I lay down my life for the sheep. (John 10:11-15)**

The book of **Genesis** describes the scene with the man Adam in the Garden of Eden; he was naming the animals, walking in authority and fellowshipping with God. The Bible never spoke of Satan neither a serpent being in the garden until Eve showed up. Isn't that a coincident? Satan knew that Jesus (the word of God) would be born through a woman. But, he did not know when. I can imagine the devil saying to himself, there she is; I have been waiting for her to show up. The devil have lots of patients, he knows how to wait.

Satan had some unfinished business with the woman. He was not thinking about Adam. Adam couldn't give birth, not naturally any way. It was all about the woman (the bride, the church), chosen by God who Satan knew would bring fourth a male child.

**This child will rule all nations with a rod of iron. (Revelation 12:5)**

He wanted to destroy the seed before she gave birth. For many years there has been talk about the woman being at fault by eating the forbidden fruit. But it was purpose to happen that way. It was a set up. The reason I am saying this is because, that devil stood against the woman in heaven first. He wanted to get back at the woman and her seed. He knew that the woman will give birth to a son who will rule over him. Therefore he had to devise a plan to get to the woman before she conceived so that her action will affect her seed.

There has also been talk about the man not speaking up and defending the woman. Why Adam stayed silent, I really don't know. It is questionable why Adam just watched and did not open his mouth. Could it be, he was intrigued by hearing a different voice? Or could he have been at awe because he heard a serpent speaking? We could all learn a lesson from this. We need to be cautious of who we listen to. The devil is the god of this world and the power of the air. He dominates the airwaves. Why do you think there is so many different medias. We have so many television channels we don't have time to watch. The children are occupied with video games, so that they don't have time to exercise or develop a social skill.

I would like to think that Adam was like the character Dr. Doolittle. Dr. Doolittle character was a man who spoke to the animals in their language. This of course did not matter to the devil, because he was looking for, and waiting for the woman to appear. Satan knew if he can get the woman to disobey God, he would accomplish killing or destroying her seed. When Satan tempted Eve, take note what transpired. Satan made a suggestion, causing Eve to doubt what God had said in **(Genesis 3:4) "And the serpent said unto the woman, Ye shall not surely die".** When God had already told her they will surely die, the day they eat of the tree.

When Satan challenged Eve, it caused her to second guess what God had spoken to her. He has been using this device from the very beginning. This is how doubt, unbelief, pride, lust, envy, covetous, jealousy, and everything God commanded us not to do is now come unto our human nature.

Satan is a thief, a murderer, and he comes to

steal, kill and destroy. He has done it then and he's doing this very thing today. He killed in heaven. Satan has no new tricks, **Beware**.

God taught me a very valuable lesson in the year of 2000 about the power of words. I was working at Nordstrom Distribution Center. There was a young man who was at the age of about 25 or younger, who deceived the company in order to get workman compensation by making up a story about his back being injured. As the story progressed I saw this man come in to work in a bent over position. The next time I saw him he was in a wheel chair. When I saw him in the wheel chair, he was sitting there processing some merchandise. I was walking upstairs to my department and I just so happen to glance over at him, and the Holy ghost spoke to me and said, "see him, this is what happens when a person speak a lie". He said just like a lie becomes manifested as truth, so do the truth manifest when it is spoken. I never forgot that. **Words are powerful. What you say is what you get.** I will even go further than that, **what you believe is what you receive. Jesus said it this way, "Be it unto you according to your faith".**

Satan was wrath with the woman from the beginning of time. And he was determined to destroy her. He had so much rage that the angels for-warned us of his wrath.

**Woe to the inhabiters of the earth and of the sea! For the devil is come down unto you, having great wrath, because he knoweth that he hath but a short time. (Revelation 12:12b)**

It was the woman who was going to give birth to God's word. Satan's plan was, and still is; is to persecute the woman. Women, if you want to know why you are experiencing so much pain and sorrow; it is because the devil is still mad at you and all of us. He's wrath with you (women) and your seed. Don't you dare think that you don't have to fight because Jesus has come and defeated the devil? He will not leave you alone. No, you are precious and valuable, because God is always doing a new thing and he is still birthing new things in the earth. There is always room for a deliverer. God is always raising up one every day. Look at our President Barak Obama, he's just one out of many God sent as a deliverer. You and I can be birthing greatness any day now. Say this out loud, and declare it every day, **I declare that I am pregnant with promise.** If you search the scriptures, when the children of Israel cried unto the Lord, it was the Lord who raised up a deliverer to deliver them. One book in the bible in particular that reveal God sending and raising up a deliverer over and over again is the book of Judges.

**And the dragon was wroth with the woman,**

**and went to make war with the remnant of her seed, which keep the commandments of God, and have the testimony of Jesus Christ. (Revelation 12:17)**

The devil will do everything he can to cause you grief. He can't do nothing about you receiving the blessing, he just don't want you to enjoy the blessing. God is your hiding place. No matter what Satan tried to do, it did not stop the plan of God. What he did do was cause division between the man, the woman and the family. The first thing we see happen in the garden was that Adam blamed the woman God gave him. "Ain't that a trip". When Adam ate of the fruit, his judgment was twisted. He went from being one with the woman to being divided from her and God. He became disconnected. This is one of the enemy weapons; he wants to disconnect us from God, and one another. If he can get you to disobey God, he will then make you doubt if God still loves you. The first thing Adam and Eve did was to hide from God. They had been walking with God, talking with God, and now they are afraid when God showed up to talk with them as he had done before. This is another trick of the enemy; to get you to run from God instead of to God. Listen, if you sin after being saved, REPENT, and turn to God.

Eve immediately pointed out and identified the enemy who beguiled her to eat. It is no wonder how she recognized Satan so quickly. Could it be from her having an encounter with him before, in heaven? Hmm. That's no coincident. The spirit of the woman in heaven helped Eve to identify him. We have a natural gift to discern. If you know it or not lady's we still have that gift to discern, and to identify the enemy no matter how he appears. We just need to exercise that gift.

When you have a gut feeling about something, **stop ignoring that feeling.** When you have dreams about something and you wake up from your dream feeling like something is wrong, don't disregard those feelings. God have given us something that men don't have, and that is inside information, some call it a woman's intuition. Please understand men have inside information when they have a relationship with God, but it is not like a women's relationship with God. We have something special with him. A woman was in the mind of God from the beginning. He knew just how he was going to carry out his plan. Only God can think to create a thing that will produce and reproduce without having to do it again.

God spoke to man on earth first to set up his plan. He made him in his image, expecting him to be like him. But, it was a woman who he entrusted to deliver his word. Don't get me wrong, we have many anointed men of God out there preaching the word with power.

But, it is something about a woman who have a womb. It is not the womb that makes us who we are; it is the impartation imparted in us from God. He fashioned us as his own bride. There's a reason why there are so many women in the churches. Women are natural worshipers.

Listen up ladies, if you are being mistreated by someone; know that you deserve better. You are royalty. God loves you so much, and he cares so much for you that he calls himself your husband.

**(Isaiah 54:5)** says, **For thy Maker is thine husband; the Lord of hosts is his name; and thy redeemer the Holy One of Israel; The God of the whole earth shall he be called.**

After Adam and eve ate the forbidden fruit they were driven out of the garden of Eden. It seemed to me like this happened before in heaven when Satan was cast out. The devil lost his place in heaven and he wants you to lose your place there too. The result from Adam and Eve's action showed me how our actions can cause you to lose your place in God. Anytime Satan can get you to disobey God, he causes you to lose your place in God. I say in God, because God is our hiding place. When we fellowship with God, and obey him we are able to hear his instructions, and his guidance. When we sin against God, we then feel out of place, and it opens the door for Satan to come in your space to cause you to feel guilty, and condemned.

After Adam and Eve were sent out of the garden, they knew each other in a sexual way. When the two had sexual relation, their children were now born in the sinful state that they were in. They passed on to their children the spirit of disobedience. Their seed was now taunted with the spirit of Satan, the spirit to kill, to steal and to destroy. This example is not only true for that time, it is still true today. You have heard of spiritual blessing, and spiritual curses.

**"What you decide to do now will make a difference later. The choices you make today can and will have an effect on your children".**

Eve gave birth to two sons. The oldest was Cain and the younger was Abel. The spirit of jealousy rose up in Cain's heart against his brother Abel and killed him. This murdering spirit that was in Cain is still working in our children today. Every time we see killings happening around us.

We are all God's children, created in his image, and from the beginning of creation he told us to be fruitful and to multiply and to have dominion over the fouls of the air and the fish of the sea and every creeping thing. Not one another.

# THE BEGINNING

(Galatians 3:26,27) says, for ye are all the children of God by faith in Christ Jesus. For as many of you as have been baptized into Christ have put on Christ.

For ye are all the children of God by faith in Christ Jesus. (Galatians 3:26)

Sadly to say some of God's children has fallen under the power of darkness when they chose to disobey God, and they are now under the influence of Satan, therefore they are not counted among the children of God. The reason why they are not the children of God is because they have rejected God's only begotten son Jesus Christ the one he sent to save and deliver them. It is sad that some do love evil more than they love good.

We too were once under the devil's influence until we came into the knowledge of God. The same spirit that was operating in Satan, is now operating in our children. The spirit of disobedient originated from Satan. He is known as the father of lies. He comes to steal, kill, and destroy. But Jesus has come so that we may have life, and to have it more abundantly. We have the power to choose who we are going to believe and serve. We have to declare God's word against the enemy's word. **Open Your Mouth and Speak what God said.** Stop giving the devil permission to defeat you by agreeing with the devil's words. When that devil show up rather it is by Doctor, sickness, or diseases, you then say out of your own mouth you are healed. **Say what God said.**

We have the power ladies and gentlemen to defeat the enemy no matter what he does. God is on our side, and he have favored us and don't you forget it. He has promised that we shall bruise Satan's head and he shall bruise our heal. The only thing you should be getting from Satan is a sore heal from stomping his head, giving him a massive headache. Understand where Satan is, he is under your feet. Every now and then he will raise up his head, and I can attest to this in my own personal life.

On September 4, 2002 I had a dream, in my dream I was walking and I looked down on the ground and I saw this beautiful blue and black shinning thing, and I said ooh look isn't that pretty. And when I said that the blue and black thing began to move and it raised itself up above my head and I yelled out it's a snake. I then began to run pass the dragon, but the dragon swooped down and bite me on my neck. I am using the word dragon because this snake was huge. When it bite me, my neck swelled up really big. Remember now this was only a dream. But the realization was that God was revealing to me who had rose up against me. That devil who has great wrath stands against us and our seed (children) is fighting us in hope to discourage our faith. I admit it shook me for a moment before the Holy Spirit kicked in to settle my Spirit. The Holy Spirit spoke to my spirit and reminded me of the time when the snake bite Paul. **(Acts 28:3-6) says, And when Paul had gathered a bundle of sticks. And laid them o the fire, there came a viper out of the heat, and fastened on his hand. And when the barbarians saw the venomous beast hang on his hand, they said among themselves, No doubt this man is a murderer, whom, though he hath escaped the sea, yet vengeance suffereth not to live. And he shook off the beast into the fire, and felt no harm. Howbeit they looked when he should have swollen, or fallen down dead suddenly; but after they had looked a great while, and saw no harm come to him, they changed their minds, and said that he was a god.**

So, my mind began to think, as I lay there; okay, the snake bite Paul and he shook it off and the people said he must be a god. My spirit was settled and I continue to sleep but pondered on it when I awake that morning. I immediately pleaded the blood of Jesus over my children and I asked God to place a hedge of angels all around them. And I also wasn't sure if God was forewarning me about something happening to me. After all, the snake bit me in my dream. I thought to myself; and I question God; I asked Lord am I going to get sick? I just didn't know at that time what the dream had meant. What I did know was that the devil was involved, and he was going to attack somewhere. I dreamt this dream on a Wednesday. My son was shot on a Sunday, September 8, 2002 around 8:00 p.m. He was shot once in the chest by a young man who was 15 yrs. The young man approach my son and the two of them got into an altercation. The young man pulled out a gun and shot my son once in the chest and he was pronounced dead at United Medical Center in S.E. Washington D.C. formerly known as Greater S.E. Hospital. Let me just say this about the young man that shot my son. This was not the first time the two of them had met. The first time my **son came across** this young man was a few months prior to the shooting. The young man had approach my son one day as my son was going to the home of his baby mama's house. The young man approach my son by way of asking him what was he doing around here? My son made it known to the young man that he was not a punk and that he was not intimidated by his approach. As time went on, and at the opportune time, he approaches my son again. This time would be the last.

My phone rang several times, in hope to reach me. I never answered the phone. Because I thought it was someone calling for my middle son Jeff; who wasn't home at the time. I then received a knock at the door, a banging on the door. It was my niece who franticly told me that my son is dead. I responded by saying; NO HE'S NOT. I got on the phone to call my son's girlfriend whose house he was over when I saw him last. I wanted to know where my son was. She said that she didn't know. I left my house and drove to the hospital. I think I drove to Prince Georges Hospital first before driving to United Medical Center formerly known as Greater S.E. Community Hospital. When I arrived at the hospital where he was pronounced dead, they put me in a small room. A nurse came in the room, and said that they have taken my son to the morgue. She said that my son was shot once in the chest, and she said if it will help he didn't bleed much. She tried to give me the news as tender as possible. I'm sure she said more, but I strictly remember that one thing. I called my grandson's grandmother Avera, because I had taken my grandson to my son earlier that day, and I wanted to make sure he had gotten home safely.

When I think back to the moment of seeing my son for the last time; I remember having my grandson at my house, and my grandson would say to me and kept saying I want to see my daddy. This was on a Saturday. I was doing someone's hair, and the time that I finish the person hair it was too late to take my grandson to see his dad. My son didn't have a car at that time. My grandson and I went to church the following morning, and again my grandson said franticly; "I want to see my dad". He said it in a desperate tone. I drove to my son girlfriend's house where he was staying and dropped my grandson off to him. And as I walked away from my son, I remember glancing back to look at him and I thought to myself he needs a haircut.

When I called my grandson's grandmother I told her what had happened, and she met me at the hospital; from there we went to the morgue in S.E. Washington, it was near the D.C. General Hospital. By the time we got to the morgue it was after 1:00 a.m. The morgue was closed. I didn't care. I wanted to see my son. I banged and banged on the door, until a female security guard opened the door. She answered with a confused look as if to say lady why are you banging on the door like this. She said maim we are closed; you will have to come back in the morning. I shouted at her and said, **"WHERE IS MY SON". I WANT TO SEE MY SON** I shouted. She softly said maim, I'm sorry I'm just security, they're close you will have to come back in the morning. She explained that she couldn't help me or do anything because they were close. I then went home. I did not sleep all night. I did ask God where was his angels? He gave me my answer later, I will tell you later in the book.

Early that morning I called my girlfriend Shona Fields. She and her husband were Pastoring their own church called Chosen Ministry International. She told me that she and her husband will go with me to identify the body. She said that if God still have work for him to do on earth, then God will raise him back up. On our way to the morgue her husband would say to me **"only believe"**. When he said that, I thought to myself I do believe, "I didn't want to hear that"; **I wanted to hear that Jesus stop the funeral.** The reason I thought this way is because I remembered a sermon preached on this subject. The sermon came out of the book of Luke. It is a story about Jesus raising a widow woman's son. And it reads: **And it came to pass the day after, that he (Jesus) went into a city called Nain; and many of his disciples went with him, and much people. Now when he came nigh to the gate of the city, behold, there was a dead man carried out, the only son of his mother, and she was a widow; and much people of the city was with her.**

**And when the Lord saw her, he had "compassion on her, and said unto her, "WEEP NOT".**

**And he came and touched the bier "(casket)"; and they that bare him stood still. And he said, YOUNG MAN, I SAY UNTO THEE, "ARISE".**

**And he that was dead sat up, and began to speak. And he delivered him to his mother.**

It is these kind of scriptures that helps you get through your own life's challenges. I was already strong in faith; I didn't feel the need to be told to believe. **I believe God, no matter what.** I don't like being weak when I am challenged. Whenever I am challenged with something; something rises up in me, and all of a sudden I am not afraid but bold. I am ready to fight when situation presents itself to me as a threat. I have always been like that. I have always been a fighter.

When we entered inside the building I asked if I could see my son. The personnel handed me a clipboard with a form and a faced down photo of my diseased son. I was at awe. I was like; "what"? I looked at Pastor Ervin as to say what am I to do now? I was expecting to see my son's body; not a photo. I didn't look at the picture, I handed the photo to my grandson's grandmother Avera. She looked at the picture and then at me and nodded her head to say yes. She handed it back to me, and I still did not look at it. I handed the picture to my middle son Jeffery. He looked at the picture and nodded his head to say yes. I took the picture from his hand and I then looked at the picture; and I remember thinking to myself "he looks as if he's asleep". The personnel then ask me to sign a form to confirm that I have identified the body. I was so disappointed that I could not physically see my son. I looked at my girlfriend husband Pastor Ervin, and asked him what we going do. I was expecting to see my son. Pastor Ervin said lets pray. He prayed something. I wasn't satisfied with his prayer. When he finished praying I then prayed; and I prayed, **Father in the name of Jesus, I call my son Gregory Meredith forth right now in the name of Jesus.** I said Lord as you had raised Lazarus from the grave by calling him forth; I call Gregory forth in the name of Jesus.

I then ask the personnel person who handed me the picture a question. I asked him where is my son? He looked at me with a puzzle look on his face. I said to him, describe the place where he is. He looked at me with strange look on his face as if to say why is she asking me this? , and he said, do you really want to know. I said yes, describe it to me. He said, your son is in a room on a shelf that is stacked up on top of each other. I then asked him if my son can get out.

He had a look on his face as to say again why is she asking me this? I then asked him is the door unlocked. Again he looked confused as to why am I asking him this. I said to him if my son wanted to get out can he get out? He looked at me again with a strange look, and he said yes, he can get out. I told him, well **"Don't be surprise if you see somebody walking around here who you thought was dead".** I meant what I said. Faith comes by hearing, and hearing by the word of God. I don't believe I would have handled the death of my son if I had not been developed in God's word. When you stay in God's word, he will speak to you through his word. It pays to stay in his word, because God's word will help you through anything.

I tell you this story with peace in my spirit and soul, because God have given me the victory and my son the victory even in this. You see my son died in Christ Jesus, he was saved, and therefore he has eternal life. Let me share something else with you concerning how God prepared me for his death. It was two weeks before my son's death when I was reading the book of (**1 Thessalonians 4:13-18** and it reads: **I would not have you to be ignorant brethren concerning them which are asleep, that you sorrow not, even as others which have no hope. For if we believe that Jesus died and rose again, even so them also which sleep in Jesus will God bring with him.**

**For this we say unto you by the word of the Lord, that we which are alive and remain unto the coming of the Lord shall not prevent them which are asleep. For the Lord himself shall descend from heaven with a shout with the voice of the archangel, and with the trump of God; and the dead in Christ shall arise first. Then we which are alive and remain shall be caught up together with them in the clouds, to meet the Lord in the air: and so shall we ever be with the Lord. Wherefore comfort one another with these words.**

When reading those words I never felt so great

of peace and comfort. I thought "wow"! I've never heard this scripture spoken before. I have always heard people quote at funerals:

**(John 14:1-3)** Jesus said **"Let not your heart be troubled: you believe in God, believe also in me". In my Father's house are many mansions: if it were not so, I would have told you. I go to prepare a place for you, I will come again, and receive you unto myself; that where I am, there you will be also.**

I had never heard **(1 Thessalonica 4:13-18)** spoken nor read. It jumped out of the page at me; it was a light unto me. I placed a yellow sticky in my bible on that chapter's verse, and I thought to myself that I would minister this word to someone else. I did not know that that person would be me.

This scripture comforted me, and it helped me get through that time of my bereavement. I am so grateful to God for loving me so much to send his word and healed me. I thank God for the dream he sent me, to let me know that Satan was behind it. You see sometimes a person can loose a love one and become angry with God, yes God does give life and he also can take it away but who are we to judge the living God. We are all here for a time, and yes; our life must come to an end only on this side because God promise that we shall live forever. **(Hebrews 9:23)** says, **And as it**

**is appointed unto men once to die, but after this the judgment.**

I said earlier that I ask God where was my angels. He answered me a few days after my son's death when I was in Bible College. I was taking a Bible doctrine class taught by my Co-Pastor Susie Owens at Greater Mt. Calvary Holy Church in Washington D.C. She was teaching on good and evil angels. She said that when a person dies in Christ the angels of God carries them away in Abraham's bosom or to a holding place. This answered my question about where my angels were. My angels were still working on my behalf by carrying away my son, and keeping him from the evil one. Thank You God for your faithfulness.

There is a peace and an assurance when you know and believe the promises of God. Your faith is strengthened by knowing and understanding that God is God and he will do what he said he would do; even when the circumstances or situation looks and feels entirely opposite from what God have spoken. The devil may have raised his head up, and bite me in the process, but I still believed God. It was the word of God that sustained me through it all.

Cain was the first born of Adam and Eve. No one had to teach Cain to be jealous, envious, covetous, and a murderer. He was born with the characteristic of Satan, and so is the entire world affected by the first committed sin. Cain committed the first murder. He killed his own brother Abel. Abel was a just man, a shepherd boy. He had the characteristic of Adam before the fall. I can imagine him working out there in the field with the sheep, and God talking with him as he did Adam. As Abel worked and talked with God, the spirit of jealousy rose up in Cain to kill him.

He was jealous of the relationship Abel had with God. Just like Satan is jealous of you and my relationship with God.

The human population increased upon the earth, and so did the wickedness. The earth became corrupt before God, and filled with violence. And God was displeased with man. He then decided to destroy all creation, except Noah and his family.

**And it came to pass, when men began to multiply on the face of the earth, and daughters were born unto them.**

**That the sons of God saw the daughters of men that they were fair; and they took them wives of all which they chose.**

**And the Lord said, "My spirit will not always strive with man, for that he also is flesh: yet his days**

shall be a hundred and twenty years.

There were giants in the earth in those days; and also after that, when the sons of God came into the daughters of men, and they bare children to them, the same became mighty men which were of old, men of renown.

And God saw that the wickedness of man was great in the earth, and that every imagination of the thoughts of his heart was only evil continually.

And it repented the Lord that he had made man on the earth, and it grieved him at his heart.

And the Lord said, I will destroy man whom I have created from the face of the earth; both man, and beast, and the creeping thing, and the fowls of the air; for it repenteth me that I have made them.

But Noah found grace in the eyes of the Lord. (Genesis 6:1-8)

God gave instructions to Noah to build an Ark large enough for Noah, Noah's wife, his three sons; Shem, Ham and Japheth; and their three wives; and every kind of animals male and females, to keep seed alive upon the earth. God had warned Noah that he was sending a flood that will destroy all life on the earth.    Noah was obedient to God's instruction.  God had promised Noah that he will establish a covenant with him.

It came to pass when God caused it to rain for forty days and forty nights.  And every living thing upon the earth that was not in the safety of the ark was destroyed.    The water prevailed for one hundred and fifty days.  God remembered Noah and caused a wind to pass over the earth causing the ark to come to a rest.  After several months had pass, God spoke to Noah instructing him to leave the ark.  When Noah obeyed God by going forth out of the ark, Noah offered a burnt offering on the altar to the Lord.  And his offering was pleasing to the Lord.

**And Noah build an altar unto the Lord; and took of every clean beast, and every clean fowl, and offered burnt offerings on the altar.**

**And the Lord smelled a sweet savor; and the Lord said in his heart, I will not again curse the ground any more for man's sake; for the imagination of man's heart is evil from his youth; neither will I again smite any more everything living, as I have done.**

**While the earth remaineth, seedtime and harvest, and cold and heat, and summer and winter,**

**and day and night shall not cease. (Genesis 8:20-22)**

And the Lord blessed Noah and his sons, and said unto them, **"Be fruitful, multiply, and replenish the earth**. God repeated himself again to Noah and his sons and said, **"Be fruitful, multiply; bring forth abundantly in the earth, and multiply therein"**. God meant what he said. He wants us to increase more and more. God has not change his mind concerning the blessing of his people. Hear now his promise.

**And God spoke unto Noah, and to his sons with him, saying, "And I, behold, I establish my covenant with you, and with your seed after you;**

**And with every living creature that is with you, of the fowl, of the cattle, and of every beast of the earth with you, from all that go out of the ark, to every beast of the earth.**

**And I will establish my covenant with you; neither shall all flesh be cut off any more by the waters of a flood; neither shall there anymore be a flood to destroy the earth.**

**And God said, "This is the token of the covenant which I make between me and you and every living creature that is with you, for perpetual generations".**

**I do set my bow in the cloud, and it shall be for a token of a covenant between me and the earth.**

**And it shall come to pass, when I bring a cloud over the earth, that the bow shall be seen in the cloud.**

**And I will remember my covenant, which is between me and you and every living creature of all flesh; and the waters shall no more become a flood to destroy all flesh.**

**And the bow shall be in the cloud; and I will look upon it, that I may remember the everlasting covenant between God and every living creature of all flesh that is upon the earth.**

**And God said unto Noah, This is the token of the covenant, which I have established between me and all flesh that is upon the earth.**

My hope in writing this book is to inform you readers that God's promises is for all of us who is alive today, and his promises will continue even after we are gone. It is my hope that you will understand that everything that affected our ancestors back then had an effect on us now. How? We inherited the blessings and the curses, because we were the seeds inside of them (Adam and Eve). It is sad to say that many of God's people do not know their rights to the promise. We have an inheritance left to us, that if we are not mature enough to receive it, we will forfeit what belong to us. **Now I say, that the heir, as long as he is a child, differeth nothing from a servant, though he be lord of all. (Galatians 4:1)**

Yes, there is no difference. If someone left you a million dollars, and you don't know how to retrieve it, what use will it be to you? Learn to get what belongs to you by studying the scriptures for yourself. **God has already said it was yours; it belongs to you, all you have to do is possess it.** God told this very thing to the children of Israel. He told them that he had already given them the land; all they had to do was to go in and possess the land.

When God spoke his word; his word never once returned back to him void. His word went out and performed the very thing that he had spoken. Words are a living thing. When words are spoken, words perform the thing that was spoken. I said earlier that words are powerful. Everything begins with a spoken word. **(John 1:1-3) says, In the beginning was the word, and the word was with God, and the word was God. The same was in the beginning with God. All things were made by him; and without him was not anything made that was made.**

# THE BEGINNING

If you are going to live a victorious life, you will have to take God at his word. God promised that he will bless us. The only requirement for you is to "**Believe**" that God is faithful who promised. He promised Abraham that he will have a son, and that he will make him the father of all nations. And all the families of the earth are blessed because of this.

# THE PROMISE

A Promise is a contract of an agreement made by someone who is committed to perform what was stated. The person, who makes the promise to do something, is the person who holds up the end of their bargain. When a promise is made to you, you can count on it being done. On this life journey God has given us everything we need to sustain us. He made us a promise. And he is committed to his promise to us. You will just have to trust him, and you will need to Know that whatever God said, he will surely bring it to pass. God has promise that he will never leave you nor forsake you. There are times when you do not feel God's presence, but by faith you have to continue to believe he's there, he is always with you. If you will just understand that this entire walk in life is a faith walk. For without faith it is impossible to please God. In order for you to know what faith is; you will need to know what the word of God say about you, and your circumstances. Knowing God's word; and trusting that he is faithful to perform his word will empower you to stand against all odds.

When God appeared to Abraham in **(Genesis 12)** He instructed him to get out of his country, and from his kindred, and from his father's house, unto a land that God will show him. And God told him that he will make of him a great nation, and he will bless him, and make his name great; and he shall be a blessing: And God said he will bless those that bless him, and curse those that curse him; and in him shall all families of the earth be blessed.

When God spoke to Abraham; Abraham did not ask any questions. He obeyed God the moment he spoke to him. This is a challenge for most of us. Because most of the time we are so tied to people that when God speak directly to us, we either tell someone about it and they then changes our mind cause nine out of ten they cannot hear what you hear. Another thing that will happen when God speak directly to you; You have people getting mad with you and talking against you, because they don't understand that you are obedient to the God you hear. Your nay sayer will always say to you, "That is not God". People always want you to follow them more than you following God. Besides, every person wants to be a leader and never a follower. Watch that crab in the barrel mentalities (controlled by Satan). Remember Satan introduced the crab in the barrel mentality first, when he caused the angels to fall with him, and causing them to lose their place in heaven.

**"As I said before, we are connected one to another in such a way that what you choose to do today will affect your tomorrow".**

All throughout history every one of us has experience the blessings and curses that has been pass down from our ancestors. Knowing our history is important; because we then discover the how, what, when and where about the blessings or curses extended from. The Bible is the best history book you will ever read. Every story reveals the beginning of everything. If you want to learn what God sounds like when he speak; pickup his written word and learn how he spoke to our ancestors in time past. Then will you hear him for yourself. God speaks to you through his written word. Once you spend time in the word you become familiar with God, and how he speak, and then you will hear him audibly.

When God spoke to Abram, he obeyed God. His obedience to God led me to believe that his father Terah taught him something about God in order for Abram to hear and know God's voice. Abram left Haran along with his wife Sarai, and their servants and his nephew Lot went with them.

Abram past through the land of Canaan, to a place called Sichem unto the plain of Moreh. And the Lord appeared to Abram again and said, **"Unto thy seed will I give this land"**. And Abram built an altar there in honor of the God who appeared to him, and he continued south on his journey. Please understand something about God. When God makes a promise he honors that promise even when the person he promised it to is dead and gone.

Abram was very rich in cattle, silver, and in gold. And Abram's nephew Lot was also rich in substance that the land was not able to bear them both. And it came to past that there was strife between the herdmen of Abram's cattle and the herdmen of Lot's cattle. And Abram said unto Lot, let there be no strife between us; for we are brothers. He says to Lot, this whole land is big enough for the both of us, separate yourself from me, if you take the left, then I will take the right. And the two separated themselves. Lot journeyed east and pitched his tent toward Sodom, and Abram dwelled in the land of Canaan.

After Lot separated from Abram, the Lord spoke to Abram and said:

**Lift up now. thine eyes, and look from the place where thou art northward, and southward, and eastward and westward; For all the land which thou seest, to thee will I give it, and to thy seed forever.**

**And I will make thy seed (descendants) as the dust of the earth: so that if a man can number the dust of the earth, then shall thy seed also be numbered.**

**Arise, walk through the land in the length of it and in the breath of it; for I will give it unto thee. (Genesis 13:14-17)**

God continue to speak to Abram time and time again, he told Abram over and over again that he was going to bless him and his seed. After several events transpired in the life of Abram the Lord appeared again unto Abram in a vision saying, **Fear not, Abram; I am thy shield, and thy exceeding great reward.** But Abram challenged God by asking him what he will give him seeing that he have no children. He then asked God will he inherit the child born in his house from his servants. God replied to him saying no, your child shall come forth out your own bowels. God told Abram if he can number the stars so shall his seed be. And the bible says that Abram believed God, and he counted it to him for righteousness.

# THE PROMISE

When Abraham received this promise that he would have a child in his old age he was seventy five years old. The promise did not manifest until some twenty-five years later. Yet the Bible says that Abraham believed God. It was Sarah who suggested to Abraham to take her handmaid Hagar for his wife. She knew in her heart that her husband wanted a son, and she thought that it would be impossible to give him a baby in her old age.

God allowed Abraham to have sexual relation with Hagar, and he also allowed Hagar to become pregnant. I said allowed because God did not interfere. He does not over ride our will, but he will keep certain things from happening. I just believe, and this is just me, when we attempt to do things against the word of God, I believe that what we attempt to do is still in God's plan because he already knew the decision we would make, because he knows us. He knows our thoughts from afar off. Meaning, before it even enters our mind, God knows. Nothing surprises God. What I like about God he still will perform what he had promised.

When you are willing, believing, and submitting to God's will, he is faithful to carry out his promise. God do not waste his time with someone who is not receptive to his word. But, he is faithful to his word.

The Bible said that Sarah did not conceive until

her menstrual cycle had stopped. What I like about God is that he will perform his word after you have tried everything in your own power to make it work. God does not do things in our timing, but in his own timing. When God revealed his promise to Sarah that she was going to conceive she laughed, and the Lord said to Abraham why did Sarah laugh, **is there any thing too hard for God?**

Many of us have yet to grasp the concept of taking God at his word. If you search throughout history, when God said a thing, it happened. It did not always happen when he spoke it, but eventually it did happen. God's plan and purpose is always fulfilled in its time. In the book of **(Ecclesiastes 3:1)** it says, **"To everything there is a season, and a time to every purpose under the heaven.** God determines the time, season, and purpose". We sometimes want things to happen when we want it to happen, and we can't figure out why it's not happening. **It is not time yet. (Daniel 2:21) says, God changes the times and the seasons:**

Sarah knew that her husband wanted a son, and she was not able to give him one, so she thought. She did not know that God had in mind for her to conceive. She then thought of a way to give her husband a son by using her handmaid Hagar. Isn't this just like us humans? Always wanting to help God; instead of letting God do it in his own timing. We have a tendency to try to make things work according to our plan. And then when things don't work out we want to cry out to God and ask him why did such and such a thing happen? It happened because you got in the way.

What I like about God is that he makes room for us to grow. When God chose us, he already knew what he was getting. Nevertheless, he is so patient with us. On the other hand, Sarah did not know that she gave birth to a spirit that will affect all other women. Sarah and many other women fail to realize that whatever decision they make, and whatever choices they choose, will affect the next generation.

If any of you women are asking the question why is it so easy for another woman to sleep with your husband, ask no further. Your mother Sarah gave every women permission when she gave Hagar permission to sleep with her husband. The scripture says that once Hagar became pregnant, she despised Sarah. **(Genesis 16:5,6)** says, **And Sarai said unto Abram, my wrong be upon thee: I have given my maid into thy bosom: and when she saw that she had conceived, I was despised in her eyes: the Lord judge between me and thee. But Abram said unto Sarai, Behold, thy maid is in thy hand; do to her as it pleaseth thee. And when Sarai dealt hardly with her, she fled from her face.** Hagar did run from the situation, but the Lord helped Hagar. God spoke to her through an angel to encourage her to return.

**(Genesis 16:9-11)** says, **And the angel of the Lord said unto her, Return to thy mistress Sarai. I will multiply thy seed exceedingly, that it shall not be numbered for multitude. And the angel of the Lord said unto her, Behold, thou art with child, and shalt bear a son, and shalt call his name Ishmael; because the Lord hath heard thy affliction. And he shall be a wild man; his hand will be against every man, and every man's hand against him; and he shall dwell in the presence of all his brethren.**

Isn't this just like God. He steps in right on time. God is not a God of confusion. He had a plan for Hagar and her son. You see a lot of times we stress out about things we don't understand. "Nothing just happens". God did not allow Hagar and her son to suffer for the action of Sarah. Besides, Hagar and her child was a part of God's plan. God promised that he would multiply Abraham's seeds. Therefore, because Ismael too is now Abraham's seed he too is blessed. I didn't say it, God said it.

At the appointed time God appeared again to Abram, and he spoke to Abram concerning changing his name from Abram to Abraham. **(Genesis 17:5)** says, **Neither shall thy name any more be called Abram, but thy name shall be Abraham; for a father of many nations have I made thee.** Whenever God is about to do something, he will call a thing something before it becomes what he said. After his name was change, God told Abraham again that his wife will conceive a son. God then instructed Abraham to no longer call his wife's name Sarai, but Sarah, for she shall be the mother of nations. **(Genesis 17:15,16)**

God sent angels to Abraham again to inform him that they will return again according to the time of life. Sarah over heard them and laughed within herself. The angels perceived her thoughts and looked to Abraham and asked, **"Is there anything too hard for God"?** And the Lord visited Sarah and she conceived and gave birth to a son at 90 years old just as he had spoken. Abraham was a hundred years old when Isaac his son from his wife was born.

After the birth of Isaac, Ishmael the son of Hagar began to make fun of Sarah's son. Sarah was displeased by his action so that she then ordered her husband Abraham to throw them both out. This decision Abraham had to make was not easy. The reason I say this is because God said to Abraham, **"Let it not be grievous in thy sight because of the lad, and because of the bond woman; in all that Sarah hath said unto thee, hearken unto her voice; for in Isaac shall thy seed be called. And also of the son of the bond woman will I make a nation, because he is thy seed. (Genesis 21:12,13)**

# THE PROMISE

Abraham sent his son Ishmael and Hagar his mother away with a bottle of water to drink and bread. The amount of bread is undetermined. Whatever the amount was, it was used up in no time as they wondered in the wilderness. Hagar became wearied and tired. She did not know what she would do now that there was not any more bread to eat or water to drink. She thought to herself to leave the child, because she didn't want to watch her child die from starvation. What can a mother do, when she's faced with not being able to provide for her child? The Bible said that she sat down a little ways off from the child, lifted up her voice and wept.

When you are faced with not knowing what to do, the only best thing to do is to cry out to God. God is merciful and compassionate. Hagar might be a bond woman, but God is merciful to the bond and the free. The Scripture says that he rains on the just and the unjust. And he shall show mercy unto whomsoever he pleases.

The Scripture goes on to say that God heard the voice of the child.

**And God heard the voice of the lad; and the angel of God called to Hagar out of heaven, and said unto her, what aileth thee, Hagar? Fear not; for God hath heard the voice of the lad where he is.**

# THE PROMISE

**Arise, lift up the lad, and hold him in thine hand; for I will make him a great nation.**

**And God Opened her eyes, and she saw a well of water; and she went, and filled the bottled with water, and gave the drink.**

**And God was with the lad; and he grew, and dwelt in the wilderness, and became an archer. And he dwelt in the wilderness of Paran; and his mother took him a wife out of the land of Egypt. (Genesis 21:17-21)**

God is a merciful God. He hears the cries of his children, and his plans and purpose for us never fails. He did not suffer the child of Hagar to suffer from the wrong of Sarah. God is that same way today. When we are faced with difficult decision, and we don't know what to do God always shows up just in time.

God blessed Ishmael with twelve sons and then Ishmael died at the age of one hundred and thirty-seven years old.

Isaac Abraham's son of the promise married Rebekah and she gave birth to twin boys Jacob and Esau. Jacob loved Esau, and Rebekah loved Jacob. Esau being the first born was entitled to the blessing that were to be passed down by his father. But Jacob and his mother Rebekah plotted against him. Jacob first tricked his older brother Esau out of his birth right, and later deceived their father by pretending to be Esau. Jacob received the blessing from his instead of Esau. This caused Esau to be furious with Jacob that he wanted to kill him. Jacob fled from Esau to his uncle Laban's house. Laban had two daughters Rachel and Leah. Jacob married them both. Jacob loved Rachel and hated Leah; this caused God to open Leah's womb and she conceived. The relationship between the two sisters was an ongoing competition. It had gotten so bad between them that they both gave their handmaiden to their husband to sleep with; and to have children. There were a total of thirteen children born unto them; twelve sons and one daughter. God later changed Jacob's name from Jacob the deceiver and trickster to Israel meaning "Prince with God". God kept his promises to Abraham by blessing his son Isaac, and all children born after him. Jacob and Esau both grew into being very prosperous men. We are still reaping the blessings from the promise made to Abraham, Isaac, and Jacob. We too are Abraham's seed by faith.

Please understand that God had planned for us to be blessed before the foundation of the world. He has been setting things into place from the beginning of time. His plan for us began in heaven, when he envisioned a woman giving birth to our savior.

# THE PROMISE

Therefore from the beginning of time before Eve gave birth to Cain, Able, and Seth she and every woman after her had an expectation to give birth to a deliverer. After Adam and Eve ate of the forbidden fruit and God asked them what they have done. The man blamed the woman and the woman exposed that serpent the devil. It was the woman who revealed who was responsible for their disobedience. Now after God had heard from the both of them; God spoke and said,

**And the Lord God said unto the serpent, Because thou hast done this, thou also art cursed above every beast of the field; upon thy belly shalt thou go, and dust shalt thou eat all the days of thy life.**

**And I will put enmity between thee and the woman, and thou shall bruise thy head, and thou shalt bruise his heel.**

**Unto the woman he said, I will greatly multiply thy sorrow and thy conception: in sorrow thou shalt bring forth children; and thy desire shall be to thy husband, and he shall rule over thee.**

**And unto Adam he said, because thou hast hearkened unto the voice of thy wife, and hast eaten of the tree, of which I commanded thee, saying, thou shalt not eat of it: cursed is the ground for thy sake;**

**in sorrow shalt thou eat of it all the days of thy life;**

**Thorns also and thistles shall it bring forth to thee; and thou shalt eat the herb of the field: In the sweat of thy face shalt thou eat bread, till thou return unto the ground; for out of it wast thou taken: for dust you art, and unto dust shalt thou return. (Genesis 3:14-19)**

The curse God spoke on the woman was the exact same thing that the woman in heaven experienced, "Birth Pain".  The reason I say this is because when we saw the woman in heaven travailing with birth pain; this spoken curse was present.  I have once heard that salvation is free but the anointing will cost you something.  And that something is much pain.  But when you endure it, you bring forth much fruit.

God prophetically spoke that the woman should give birth to a seed that will bruise the devil's head and the devil will bruise his heel.

**For unto us a child is born, unto us a son is given; and the government shall be upon his shoulder; and his name shall be called Wonderful, Counselor, The Mighty God, The Prince of Peace. (Isaiah 9:6)**

Yes, God purposed to send a deliverer to us his

people on earth where the devil fell, when he from glory. The devil couldn't rule in heaven and he cannot rule on earth. God is God of the heaven and the earth. For God has given us the authority to rule and have dominion here on earth. The only power Satan have is deception. If he can get you to believe his lies, he has blinded your mind from the truth. The truth is that Jesus defeated Satan and stripped him of his authority when he died on the cross for us in our place; he took our punishment for the sins we committed, and he rose from the dead and took back everything that was lost to Adam and Eve in the garden. Jesus regained the authority and all power that was lost in the garden, and because he got it back from the devil, he has fulfilled the promise God had spoken to Eve when he promised that **the seed of the woman shall bruise the head of the devil.**

Jesus went down to hell to free the captives of those who died before his coming. He went to hell so that we will not have to go to hell. Jesus death and resurrection defeated every obstacle against us, even the strength of sin. The nature of sin is very much alive among us, but it only has power over you when you give your will over to it. **But the scripture hath concluded all under sin; that the promise by faith of Jesus Christ might be given to them that believe.** Your belief, and your knowing what Jesus accomplish for you on the cross is your weapon against the enemy that accuses us day and night. We are to walk boldly, with the assurance of our victory. For God sent his Word (son) and healed us. And that Word goes by the name of Jesus Christ.

# OBEYING GOD'S WORD

**(Genesis 12:1-3)** says, **Now the Lord had said unto Abraham, Get thee out of thy country, and from thy kindred, and from thy father's house, unto a land that I will show thee: And I will make of thee a great nation, and I will bless thee, and make thy name great; and thou shalt be a blessing: And I will bless them that bless thee, and curse him that curseth thee; and in thee shall all families of the earth be blessed.**

God called Abram apart from his father and his relative because God had a far greater plan for Abram than his relatives. This is the beginning of the promise of God spoken to Abraham over 2000 years ago, and we are still reaping the fruit. God spoke and Abraham believed God.

(Romans 4:3) says, **For what said the scripture? Abraham the father of us all, believed God, and it was counted unto him for righteousness.**

(Romans 4:20,21) said, **He staggered not at the promise of God through unbelief; but was strong in faith, giving glory to God: And being fully persuaded that, what he had promised, he was able also to perform.**

(Romans 4:16) says, **Therefore it is of faith, that it might be by grace; to the end the promise might be sure to all the seed; not to that only which is of the law, but to that also which is of the faith of Abraham; who is the father of us all.**

God has promise to bless us, and our children. God fulfilled his promise to Abraham in the appointed time and season for Sarah to become pregnant. She gave birth to Isaac. And out of Isaac was born Jacob, and out of Jacob was born the twelve tribes of Israel. God changed Jacobs name from deceiver to a prince who now have power with God and with men, and hast prevailed.

What I have learned from Jacobs name change is that, when God changed Jacobs name to Israel, he referred to all of Jacobs seed (children) as Israel. The name change fulfilled the promise that he made to Abraham that his seed shall be blessed. We are Abraham's seed according to faith. If you believe God like our father Abraham then you too are counted as his seed. Abraham begat Isaac, and Isaac begat Esau and Jacob whose name was changed to Israel. And in Israel's seeds we are blessed according to promise. God promise Abraham that he would bless his seed. Abraham is the father of all nations. He is the Father of faith. We are accounted as Abraham seed because we have been grafted into the family by faith. If you can receive this saying, than you and I and our children are a prince and princess, who now have power with God and with men, and we have prevailed. Hallelujah! In case you missed it. The name Israel means prince.

When the blessing of God is upon your life, expect others to see and take notice. People will see the blessing and become jealous. The Bible said, that when Joseph died, and a new Pharoah arouse who knew not Joseph. This Pharoah saw the increase of the children of Israel and became afraid. He said unless they rise up against us, let me be harsh with them, and make their labor hard. But, the bible said that the more they burdened them the more they increased. I need some God believing warriors who have been burdened by the Pharoah's in your life to rejoice for being a threat to your Pharaohs.

The burden of the children of Israel caused them

to mourn, and cry, that God heard them. He raised up a deliverer for them. Moses was chosen by God, to go and stand up to this mighty man (Pharaoh) who was the governor or ruler of Egypt. When God called Moses, his response was, here am I. How many of you have a "Here am I in your spirit"?

God made himself known to Moses by identifying himself as God of his ancestors, the God of Abraham, Isaac, and Jacob. God gave Moses instructions to go to Egypt to deliver the people of Israel. But Moses, like many of us had self issues. He said to God, (**Exodus 4:10**) O' my Lord, I am not eloquent, neither heretofore, nor since you have spoken unto your servant: but, I am slow of speech, and of a slow tongue. And Lord said unto him;

**Who hath made man's mouth? Or who maketh the dumb or deaf, or the seeing, or the blind: have not I the Lord? ( verse 12) Now therefore go, and I will be with thy mouth, and teach thee what thy shall say. (Exodus 4:10)**

This is for those who answered the call, and responded with here I am. God said that he will be with your mouth and he will teach you what to say. **Do you believe God today?**

The almighty God is able to exceed our

own limitation. Our flesh has its dysfunctions and inadequacy, but God who gives us the strength and confidence in him to do what we could not do in our own ability. When God speak to you individually to do something, **do it.** He who commanded you to do it will give you the grace and the ability to follow it through. It is up to you to obey God when you here him speak.

Throughout history, God has used the least, the last and the lost. He has spoken saying, he has not chose us because we were many. He didn't even choose us because we had it all together, not even half way together.

**For thou art a holy people unto the Lord thy God: the Lord thy God hath chosen thee to be a special people unto himself, above all people that are upon the earth.**

**The Lord did not set his love upon you, nor choose you, because ye were more in number than any people; for ye were the fewest of all the people:**

**But because the Lord loved you, and because he would keep the oath which he had sworn unto your fathers, hath the Lord brought you out with a mighty hand, and redeemed you out of the house of bondmen, from the hand of Pharaoh king of Egypt. (Deuteronomy 7:6-8)**

**(1 Corinthians 1:27-29)** says, **God hath chosen the foolish things of the world to confound the wise; and God hath chosen the weak things of the world to confound the things which are mighty; And base things of the world, and things which are despised, hath God chosen, yea, and things which are not, to bring to nought things that are: That no flesh should glory in his presence.**

God knows from the beginning who you are, and your capabilities when he called you. He knows what you will choose to do, before you even do it; it is still part of the plan. So many times we have messed up and thought that God couldn't forgive us for what we have done. But, he already knew what we would do. Whenever you get off the course that God has plan for you, repent, turn away from it and, turn back to God, and continue your walk with him. When you ask God for forgiveness, he forgives you and cast it into the sea of forgetfulness and, remembers them no more.

You have to forgive yourself, and move on. When you obey God it is his responsibility to get you where he will send you. It is your responsibility to seek him and listen for his instructions, and then do it. Whenever you are facing tough times just remember that the situation you are experiencing are temporal. It is doing this time when you will feel that God is not with you. It is doing this time that you will have to remember that **God is the same yesterday, today and forever. It is doing this time that you will have to take God at his word, and believe he will do just what he said. Remember that God didn't change his mind you changed yours. Get back into agreeing with God.**

When you read the stories of the lives of the people that God spoke to and chosen, you will notice that there was always some sign of doubt from the receiver. When God spoke through his angels, or his men of God, it was always a message that looked impossible to the person it was told to. Especially when you consider what God have to work with, it's really not much. Our perception only sees the limitation of this flesh. It's the flesh that works against us, the flesh and the blinding deception of the devil. The devil wants to remind you of your weak-nesses. He wants you to focus on what you can't do, and to focus on the situation at hand. I challenge you to look beyond where you are; believe what God say about the situation, and I guarantee you that God will be with you every step of the way. Don't allow this flesh to limit you. God is a Spirit, and they that worship him must worship him in Spirit and in Truth. God's Word is True.

I remember thinking to myself saying;" if this earth suit had a zipper" I would unzip it and throw it away. The reason I say this is because this flesh has been introduced to so many things, and it now has an appetite with cravings and desires. Drug addicts and alcoholics aren't the only ones with addictions. It's no wonder the bible says that in this flesh dwells no good thing. Therefore, when you are making progress to walk in the spirit, here comes that appetite of the flesh raising its ugly head. Not only does the flesh give us problems, our mind is the greatest problem. Satan is big on using what he knows about us against ourselves. We have so much information stored in the memory of our mind that I believe even when we were living in our mother's womb, we received information from her words and the words of her environment; that her very words that we heard her speak already started a way of thinking for us. **The words you hear can have an effect on you.** That's why the Bible tells us to take heed to what you hear.

You see everything starts and began with a seed. Words are seeds. The seed of your words will become what you sow. When you and I speak we speak life or death. Everything and everyone is affected by the words they hear and speak. Depending on where you been and who you been hanging around determines how much you know. The words of others have influenced the way you think and what you believe. So that when you hear God speak something contrary to what you see and know to believe, you tend to doubt. It is up to you to take hold of what God has spoken, you can have what God said you can have, and you can do what God said you can do.

What I have learned from reading the bible is that, God gave our forefathers instructions. Some obeyed the word of God and some did not. The people who did not obey, or believe died before receiving the promise. God was still with them. But because of the spirit of disobedient, the people walked according to their own lustful desire. They had a mentality of a learned way of thinking. But, those that obeyed God lived under God's protection.

You have to understand that idolatry is still alive and well this very day. When you make some other thing or some other person your idol, it becomes your god. God meant what he said that you should have no other God besides him. This world system if you really study the history of it, it has not changed. The season and times have changed, but the people are still the same. There are people who are still under the influence of Satan. Satan is still the god of this world. He is blinding the minds of the people.

If you want to know when and how something began you have to start at the beginning. (**Genesis 1:1),** In the beginning God. This is a good place to start, with God. God is the beginning of everything and everyone. Why is it that man continues to look to another man for his answer? The Bible says, in **(Jeremiah 17:5), Cursed be the man that trusts in man, and makes flesh his arm, and whose heart departs from the Lord.** Don't get me wrong we all need each other, but God wants you to look to him first and he will supply your needs. He will give you the answer you are looking for. I have personally learned that when I ask God a question he will show me the answer in His Word (Bible), or he will allow me to hear it through the man or woman of God. Let me set the record straight when I say a man or woman of God; not any man or woman of God; "Only the God chosen man or woman of God". What I mean by this is that all Pastors and preachers are not chosen by God. There are some who put themselves in those positions, and not God. I also learned that you have to have a relationship with God in order to hear from God. God's sheep knows his voice and they do follow him.

**(Note: There are many promises from God that is written in the Holy Bible. I encourage you to search the scriptures for yourself and learn all of them for yourself. Not one of his promises will fail).**

**(Isaiah 34:16) says, Seek ye out of the book of the Lord, and read: no one of these shall fail. (KJV) The message Bible says it this way. Get and read God's book: None of this is going away.**

# RELATIONSHIP

Relationship is defined in Webster Dictionary as having a connection, association, or involvement; a connection between persons by blood or marriage, an emotional or other connection between people. You cannot have a relationship with someone when there is a disconnection. God wanted a relationship with us his people from the beginning of time. He created us to have relationship with him first, and then with others. It is God who said it is not good for man to be alone. He created male and female to have relationship in a marriage covenant manner, and to be fruitful and multiply their seed upon the earth, and not apart from him.

In order for you to conceive God's word you must first be in a relationship with him. A relationship began when you spend quality time with someone. Adam's relationship started with God. God communicated with Adam. A relationship is developed when communication is formed. God approves of relationship, but not the ones which will draw you away from him. God wanted Adam to have a relationship with Eve as he had with him, "A husband and wife relationship".

**For thy Maker is thine husband; the Lord of hosts is his name; and thy redeemer the Holy One of Israel: The God of the whole earth shall he be called. (Isaiah 54:5)**

**Husbands love your wives, even as Christ also loved the church, and gave himself for it. (Ephesians 5:25)**

**So aught men to love their wives as their own bodies; He that loveth his wife loveth himself. For no man ever hated his own flesh; but nourisheth and cherisheth it, even as the Lord the church. For we are members of his body, of his flesh, and of his bones. For this cause shall a man leave his Father and Mother, and shall be joined unto his wife, and they two shall be one flesh. (Ephesians 5:28-31)**

A healthy relationship is when there is communication and fellowship. When I speak of communication I am not talking about argumentation, neither am I speaking about talking at each other. Nothing comes out of arguing but confusion and division. Communication is impartation. It is sending a message; a message that is understood and received from the sender. When Adam and his wife listened to the devil they became confused, and it caused strife among them. And most importantly it separated them from God.

God who had a relationship with them knew something was wrong because his spirit discerned the division. He knew something was wrong. He then called out to Adam, and enquired of his where about.

**And they heard the voice of the Lord God walking in the garden in the cool of the day, and Adam and his wife hid themselves from the presence of the Lord God amongst the trees of the garden. And the lord God called unto Adam, and said unto him, where art thou? (Genesis 3:8-9)**

Adam's response to God was an accusation towards the woman God gave him. He did not take responsibility for his partaking of the tree which God commanded him not to eat, neither did the woman. Because of their disobedience God pronounced a punishment for them both. Unto the woman God said, **I will greatly multiply thy sorrow and thy conception;**

in sorrow thou shalt bring forth children; and thy desire shall be to thy husband, and he shall rule over thee. And unto Adam he said, because thou hast hearkened unto the voice of thy wife, and hast eaten of the tree, of which I commanded thee, saying, thou shalt not eat of it; cursed is the ground for thy sake; in sorrow shalt thou eat of it all the days of thy life; Thorns also and thistles shall it bring forth to thee; and thou shalt eat the herb of the field: In the sweat of thy face shalt thou eat bread, till thou return unto the ground; for out of it wast thou taken; for dust thou art, and unto dust shalt thou return. (Genesis 3:16)

And to the man God said, **cursed be the ground for thy sake; in sorrow shalt thou eat of it all the days of thy life;**

**Thorns also and thistles shall it bring forth to thee; and thou eat bread, till you, return unto the ground; for out of it wast thou taken: for dust thou art, and unto dust shalt thou return. (Genesis 3:17-19)**

Adam called his wife Eve. Eve meaning mother of all living; one translation says life giver. We are nurturers by nature, and care givers. Because we have experience hurt like no other and is able to stand strong through all the pain, mistreatment, physical and verbal abuse without breaking. We are empowered to endure the test of times. We were created to be a help meet. It was God who said; **"It is not good for man to be alone; I will make you a help meet that is suitable".**

The psalmist said, delight yourself in the Lord and he will give you the desire of your heart. He is the one and the only one who gives life, and meaning to your life.

**(John 1:1-4 )– In the beginning was the Word, and the Word was with God, and the Word was God. The same was in the beginning with God.**

**All things were made by him; and without him was not any thing made that was made. In him was life; and the life was the light of men.**

If you are going to survive in this world, you must stay connected to the one who created you, even a branch disconnected from a tree cannot live. We were once disconnected from God and we were graphed in because of the Israelite's (the Jews) unbelief; the bible warns us if we are not careful we too can fall off. **Well; because of unbelief they were broken off, and thou standest by faith. Be not high minded but fear: For if God spared not the natural branches, take heed lest he also spare not thee. (Romans 11:20-21)**

**Jesus (the Word ) said, I am the vine ye are the branches; He that abideth in me and I in him, the same bringeth forth much fruit: for without me ye can do nothing. (John 15:5)**

I speak to you woman who desire to be married and I encourage you to appreciate and learn to honor your relationship with God first. **(Matthews 6:33) says, But seek ye first the kingdom of God and his righteousness and all these things shall be added unto you.**

We have a habit of trying to do things our way; when God has already given us instructions. God said, when a man finds a wife he finds a good thing: "That means that you don't have to go looking women". That man will find you. God also said, It is not good for man to be a lone; He (God) will make a help meet for you. Let God be God, he wants the best for all of us. Yes, God do want us to be happy, but who said a man will make you happy. Happiness is temporal, it's a feeling, and feelings do change all the time. God said, delight yourself in him and he will give you the desires of your heart. Don't you know that there are woman who are married and wishing they were not married. Ladies please understand when God give you a husband don't make that man your god. Everything has an expiration date on it. I feel for a woman when she loses her husband or a man who loses his wife by way of death, because then they are single again. Let your peace, your joy, and your fulfillment be in the Lord. There is nothing in this world that will satisfy you forever but God.

**God made us to be relational.** We are all so divinely connected to one another. Please understand, relationship with another person can only work when you have a relationship with God first. He will teach you all things. I love God so much, because he will teach you and show you how to do something, when you seek him and ask him for help. I love God because he shows me how much he loves me and his people.

**God is love.** When you inter into a relationship with another person, you have to understand that, that person has been affected by something in life that has caused him or her some kind of hurt. Every person on earth has been influence by someone or something. You know, we as human beings think that we are a super human savior. We think that we can fix him or her. We sometimes think that we have all the answers. I want to know when did any of us become experts, and now know more that God himself.

When you study the word of God, you will learn that every character you read about have experienced pain, hurt, sorrow, rejection, opposition, challenges, death, etc. There are no perfect people. When you meet a person and connect with them, you can be sure that, that person has his or her own personal struggles. No, you are not their answer. God is everyone's answer. **(Isaiah 54:5) says, For thy Maker is thine husband; the Lord of hosts is his name; and thy Redeemer the Holy One of Israel: The God of the whole earth shall he be called.**

Have you asked God about your relationship with the people you associate with? The ones you associate with right now. How much do you know about that person? Don't you know that God will make known to you the secret things? God will reveal to you whatever you ask; you may not receive the answer right away, but he will answer.

I will never forget the day I prayed and asked God to teach me to love. This was in the year of 2006. It was doing my prayer time with him. I was talking to God about me and my issues, and I asked him to teach me to love. God took me to the scripture **(1 John 4:18), "There is no fear in love; but perfect love casteth out fear; because fear hath torment. He that feareth is not made perfect in love".** This scripture delivered me from the fear of love. Love covers and protect, it never accuses. God is that perfect love. He commanded us to love one another. What is love? According to **(1 Corinthians 13:4-8); Charity suffereth long, and is kind; charity envieth not;**

**charity vaunteth not itself, is not puffed up.**

**Doth not behave itself unseemly, seeketh not her own, is not easily provoked, thinketh no evil; Rejoiceth not in iniquity, but rejoiceth in the truth. Beareth all things, believeth all things, hopeth all things, endureth all things.**

**Charity never faileth; but whether there be prophecies, they shall fail; whether there be tongues, they shall cease; whether there be knowledge, it shall vanish away.**

I don't know anyone who fit this description but God himself. I know some people who appear to be loving and kind; but let them get tired and fed up with you. I bet you will see another side of them. We're human, we do get tired; then there is some who has mastered this description of love and they are very meek in character, for this I do applaud them.

I have conducted some soul searching on myself, and I have discovered that my personality development is traced back to my childhood. I have learned that I lost my trust for love due to an incident I experienced as a child. This was set up by the devil.

But what he meant for evil God has made it good. I was a victim of molestation, and it affected the way I perceived relationships. I would keep others at a distant. What I have learned was that not only was I keeping people at a distant I also was keeping God at a distant. I didn't discover the dis-function in my relationship with God until I asked God to teach me to love. Love is trusting. And I have said that I trusted God, but when trouble aroused, I would panic and worry about how it will work out.

From the time I was a child my love trust was destroyed. This violation distorted my way of thinking and my perception of love. It caused a breach between me and others, and especially my Dad. Because of this traumatic experience I had a different perception on how I perceived people, places and things; even my relationship with my Dad and all the people around me. I remember my dad always being in my life, and I remember    My Dad would always make sure that I had whatever I wanted or needed. He would walk me to school and he would take me to the amusement park. He would give me money to go shopping. He was always there for me, but the issue was that I was always aloof from him and others. I didn't trust people. I was afraid.

My Dad was a good Dad, and so was my mom. I don't want to continue in my writing without acknowledging the goodness of my mom. My mom would give her last. She is a very strong woman and diligent worker. She is a woman of strength. When I think of my mom I think of Jesus who laid down his life for us. There was a book written entitled "He Chose the Nails", this book describes my mom, because she chose the nails for her children, and grandchildren. She has endured so much grief, and long suffering. My mom is now eighty-five years old and will be eighty-six by the time this book is published. My mom still gets around very well, and if her children or grandchildren call upon her she is still there to give a helping hand. From the words of the Intruders who sang the song I'll Always Love my Momma, she's my favorite girl. I too will Always Love My Momma, she's my favorite girl; she brought me in this world. A mother's love is so special, it's something that you can't describe; it's the kind of love that stays with you until the day you die. I Will Always Love My Momma.

I was a spoil child growing up because I had always gotten my way. I was very insecure too. I realized this as I got older. I believe this extended from my mom having to work and would leave me with someone else to care for me while she worked. I was told by my sister that one day my mom came home and she found a red hand print on my thigh. I was told that my complexion was light and if anyone would spank me or hit me I would bruise easily. I remember crying and screaming every time my mom would leave me with a baby sitter. I was a cry baby well up till about twelve or thirteen years old. I know y'all might be saying, "That old". Yes "That old". I told you I had issues. My older brothers and sisters were made to take me with them whenever I would cry and express that I wanted to go with them.

I was the youngest of six children; my mom was the kind of mom who let me get away with a lot of things. My dad married my mom with five children. He had two daughters himself from previous relationships; yet I was still the youngest. My mom and dad eventually separated and later divorced. I would sometimes live with my dad. I remember my dad being a giving person. He was kind and caring. I know it was hard for him to understand how to communicate with me. I know he tried everything he possibly could to help me to grow up to be an intelligent adult. I know this because he would always take the time to try and teach me, and he would always get me things that were educational. But, I didn't receive most things because there was a blockage in how I understood things and people. I am saying blockage because I believe when a child has been sexually assaulted at a very young age; and when their mind and body has been introduced to something so traumatic it will cause a shutdown in their brain. It's as if you just stop. I believe the child from that moment stop being a child. The child has now entered into adulthood without understanding the rules of adults. With this being said, the devil used this against me. I never told anyone. I held it inside, and the devil played it over and over again in my mind. Once that predator awakened my sexual appetite others followed suit right in the safety of my own home where I should have been safe. So I thought.

**NOTE:** I have chosen not to reveal the names of the persons who Satan used to kill my growing years. Mentioning their names wouldn't matter because they were only weapons used by Satan. I now know that I no longer choose to accuse or expose anyone, but I choose to cover them with the love of God and under the blood of Jesus Christ. The blood of Jesus covers a multitude of sins, even mine's. I forgive them as God has forgiven me.

Growing up in my mom's house there was always strife among us. I was afraid to ask questions because when we talked to each other it would always turn to an argument. When I would ask a question I would get a defensive response; sought of like I do now when I respond to people. Me and my sisters and brothers fought, and argued a lot. I didn't understand why it was so much division between us. When I got older I understood. I left home when I turned twenty-two. I had two sons by this time. I separated myself from my mom, sisters and brothers. We didn't talk for years. Doing the separation I was attending church and developing my relationship with God. I attended

# RELATIONSHIP

Maple Springs Baptist church for about five years before leaving to attend Galilee Baptist church. While attending Galilee Baptist church I took a class called "Self Confrontation". It caused me to confront me and the issues I had.

I was a very angry and bitter person doing my younger years. I was walking in unforgiveness. I held in a lot of hurt on the inside. I remember one day in the class we were on a chapter in the book pertaining to anger and bitterness. We gathered in a circle to pray. The anointing was so powerful it destroyed the yoke of anger and bitterness off of me. I remember how it felt. It felt like a storage trunk stored with things in it being lifted up off of my shoulders. I felt one hundred percent lighter. I was so thankful to God because I wanted to be kind to people. I didn't understand why I would try to be nice and then be angry at the same time. When I completed the class I was awarded with two certificates; one for completing the class and one for dramatic deliverance. The instructor said that she presented me with this award because there was a dramatic change in me. She said that the change was so tremendous from the way I started the class up until it ended. This was the beginning of change. "To God Be the Glory".

As time went on I then began to learn about some incidents that were hidden from me as a child.

# RELATIONSHIP

It was some secrets, and unresolved issues that were never spoken about that had caused the problems, and division among me, my siblings, and my mom. This secret caused a lot of hurt and division in the family relationship. This is not something unusual among families. It was unusual to me because I thought there was a perfect family somewhere. Nevertheless, the enemy was behind it all. We all need to recognize the enemy when he interferes with our family, and ourrelationships with others.

I don't think my dad was able to handle the division (arguing) in the household. He moved out and got his own place. But before doing so he sent me to live with my grandmother when I was about eight years old, she lived in Burlington N.J. This is where my Dad is originally from. After staying with my grandmother for about a year, I returned back home to my mom's house, and sometimes my dad's house; and then back to stay with my grandmother when I was about eleven years old. God had a plan for my life. I am so grateful for my grandmother who always sent me and my cousin Tracy to church. I got saved, and baptized at age eleven while staying with my grandmother. I also was taught how to pray. I learned the prayer, "**Now I lay me down to sleep, I pray the Lord my soul to keep, if I should die before I awake I pray the Lord my soul to take**".

When I came back home to live with my mom

again, I would say my prayers every night. And, when I was sad and when I didn't know why certain things would happen to me, I would always cry and pray to God. I didn't have anyone else to talk to but God. I didn't have a relationship with anyone who I could trust enough to be able to talk to. I might have been able to talk to my mom if she hadn't snapped at me before whenever I would ask her a question. Besides that she was always busy working. My mom would do anything for her children, but what's a mother to do when she have to work to provide for her children. Again this is not to blame anyone. I love my mom, and my mom loves me very much. With no one to talk to I learned to keep everything inside. I would always talk to God by praying the prayer I learned, and crying to him to help me through my problems. God has always been my help; he was there when no one else was there for me. It was God who knew my hurt.

As I sought God, my relationship with him grew. I believed in God, and I believed his word, but that love issue wasn't perfected in me. "Fear was dominating". It was not until about six years ago when I realized that I received and perceived God like I do man. I had the same mentality toward God as I did my earthly dad; loving him from a distant.

I liked when God was being good to me, but I didn't acknowledge his goodness in an appreciative way. I responded to God the same way I did my Dad. I don't think my dad knew how much I appreciated his love for me, because I didn't express it. My dad passed away when I was sixteen. I was pregnant with my first son doing this time. I was looking for love in all the wrong places. I wanted to love, but I was afraid. I said that I love God. But that love was limited because of how my mind processed it. I had some serious strongholds in my mind that had to come down. When God took me to the scripture (**1John 4:18**) I was convicted. It says, **"There is no fear in love; but perfect love casteth out fear; because fear hath torment. He that feareth is not made perfect in love.** I was convicted that I have not been walking in love without fear, nor did I know how to love. I realized that love began with God, and with loving yourself. God is Love.

I had to question myself, how is it possible to love others when I didn't even love myself? The devil convinced me that I was worthless and shameful. This too was the work of the devil standing against me. You remember the man possessed by legends of devils, who lived in the tomb cutting him-self. A lot of us are like that man living in the tombs. The devil will put thoughts in your mind to cause you to accuse your own self. When you accuse yourself; think bad about yourself, and talk bad about yourself; you are cutting yourself. It's called self- affliction. Satan don't need to do anything to a person once he have their mind, he already have them on automatic. If he can get you to think a certain way, and you began to believe that that's just how you are. Satan has you right where he wants you. That devil is a liar. He did this same thing to the man who was living in the tombs. The devil attacked his mind, and caused him to afflict his own self by cutting himself.

**And they came over unto the other side of the sea, into the country of the Gadarenes.**

**And when he was come out of the ship, immediately there met him out of the tombs a man with an unclean spirit; who had his dwelling among the tombs; and no man could bind him, no, not with chains:**

**Because that he had been often bound with fetters and chains, and the chains had been plucked asunder by him, and the fetters broken in pieces: neither could any man tame him.**

**And always, night and day, he was in the mountains, and in the tombs crying, and cutting himself with stones.**

This man was left alone and to himself. It's dangerous to run off and to separate yourself from others, because the enemy will use this against you.

He will make you feel like no one loves you and no one cares about you. You will eventually believe those lies because you are alone. There's a scripture in the Bible that says, "No man hates his body".

**For no man ever yet hated his own flesh; but nourishth and cherisheth it, even as the Lord the church.       (Ephesians 5:29)**

I beg the difference. There are men and women that hate their body, and themselves. When you don't love yourself; you cannot love others. When a person use drugs, drink alcohol, and abuse their body, these are signs of hating their body. That devil will make a person think they are unworthy. Don't you know that there are some beautiful women out there, who think that they are not pretty? It is some hurting people out there in this world, and I was one of them. Jesus redeemed my life from destruction, and he will do the same for you. If it had not been for Jesus, I know I would not be saved and still alive today. Thank God for Jesus.

**Note: To all of you who know me personally and is now reading this book I publicly apologize for my attitude towards you. And I ask that you will forgive me for being abrasive when responding to you as a person. I used the word abrasive because my supervisor used this word when she described**

my attitude when responding to someone at work. I knew within myself that I came off a little ruff at times when trying to defend myself, but I did not know it was offensive to others. I do acknowledge that I have a strong voice tone, and it could be offensive. I apologize to all it offends. In the meantime please be patients with me; God is still working on me and he is perfecting this thing that concerns me.

I also want to apologize to my sister Delores Adams who I have stopped talking to because of her abrasive tone of voice towards me. I would point this out to her; not knowing at the time that I too have the same problem. I would say to her, "You are like a bridle pad or sand paper which rubs a person hard". I'm finding out that the very thing that seems to be offensive to me is the very thing that I too have issues with.

I have learned that some behaviors that I had struggled with were learned behavior that took root in my subconscious, and I am learning to renew my mind from wrong thinking.

Once I had asked God to teach me to love and I confessed my faults to him. He already knew where I was missing it; but I have learned that when you acknowledge that you have a problem, then you are able to get the necessary help you need. God heard my cry and answered me. I then learned to rest in him. I whole heartedly took him at his word. I had to learn how to love according to God's definition of love, and I am still learning. I am trying to be a loving person. But I'm finding out that I cannot be everything to everybody. I am being content in the state that I'm in, and as job had spoken doing his time of testing; I say, "All the days of my appointed time will I wait, till my change come". What I recently discovered by listening to others opinion about me is that I appear to be passive to them. I have been trying to tone my attitude down, but I also need to learn to balance it. I came from being feisty to appearing to be timid. The person that knows me now, doesn't know that I once was a person who would be ready to fight at any given moment. That behavior extended from hurt. I wanted to protect myself. I realize today that there are times when my defense mechanism would still kick in, and I am offensive to others because I do come off kind of ruff; but I really don't mean to offend, if so forgive me.

I have learned that love has no fear. I have learned that peace comes with true love. I learned that love has been around me all the time and I didn't even recognize it. Love started first with God. He has always been with me. God has truly blessed me with people who have genuinely demonstrated the love of God towards me. Because his love was in them; he demonstrated his love through them to me. It was God's love for me that placed me in families of caring people, and with loving people that have loved me as if I was born in their family. But because of my dysfunctions, and inability to receive the love of God through people; I in-exchange pushed many away. I am so sorry. But God; kept loving me through it all, and didn't allow the hearts of others to harden in spite of me.

I had an earthly father who was always in my life until his passing away when I was sixteen years old. He loved me unconditionally. I miss him so much. I was unable to receive his love because of my wrong perception of love.

My grandmother, my aunts, uncles, and cousins on my dad's side of the family were so good to me. If any of you are reading this book, please forgive me for my selfish attitude. I'm not saying this to say that my family members I grew up with did not love me. They loved me the best way they knew how, and its ok; it's just that there was always a lot of arguing and fighting among us, and I don't exclude myself. I didn't understand the division among us then. But I do now. The whole household was wounded with unhealed scars, and un-forgiveness. And I came to understand as a matured spiritual adult who is really behind all of this madness. Satan has caused so much division among us all. He has caused so much division in homes, and families. He is the real accuser of the brother. I speak to every person who will read this book; I say to you that all of your sins are forgiven you. You do not have to carry any guilt, shame, regret, un-forgiveness, hurt or anything that will keep you bound. We hear so many different people tell us to let it go. "They are right". You stop growing when you get stuck by not letting things go. When you think of everything God see's and knows on a daily basis, he still accepts us and love us. He hates the sin, but he loves us. He looks beyond our faults. He sees the blood of Jesus on us. This does not mean for you to continue to do things that are dis-pleasing to God. Learn to do things God's way. God said to forgive others as he has forgiven you. He has commanded us to love our enemies, and pray for those that despitefully use you. Now I know for myself this is a tough one to do. But do it anyway even if it means staying away from that person. You don't have to stay in an abusive relationship or environment. Because there are some people who will never change. There will always be those who are under the power of the influence of the devil. Thisis just how it will be until Jesus return. You will just have to keep in mind who's working through this person's behavior. This is not to say I am making an excuse for another person's behavior, I am not. What I do know is that from the beginning of time Satan has been waging war against us. His first murder was when he moved in the heart of Cain causing him to kill Abel. If you read on in the Book of Genesis you will discover that there were violence throughout the earth, and God had to destroy the first earth because of such great evil in the earth. We need to come together and join forces by being one with God, and stop fighting against one another. We need to identify our true enemy just like Eve did in the garden. She said it was the Serpent. You know the red dragon that stood against the woman in heaven. The world portrayed him as a man in a red suit with a pick fork in his hand. No, that's not him. He's an invisible being who disguises himself inside of anything or anyone.

The truth of the matter is that God loves us with an everlasting love. His love covers all of our faults and our sins. It is his love that is revealed in us when we learn to love him first, ourselves second and then others.

Our soul is empty without God in our lives. We can search all over for love, but we can never find anyone who can fill that void in our lives.

Human relationships can end at any time. He or she will and can walk out on you. All it takes is one misunderstanding, one disagreement and he or she is out of there, sometimes it don't even take that, a person will leave or stop talking to you without giving you a reason. God's love never fails.

God demonstrated his love for us over and over again. His arms are always extended and open to us, He said, **"Come unto him who is heavy laden and I will give you rest"**. If you don't know Jesus today and you want him to come into your heart, this is a good time to say this prayer, say this out loud, say, **Lord Jesus come into my heart, I am a sinner and I want to be saved. I believe that you died and rose again and you are now sitting on the right hand of our Father in heaven making intercession for us. I am asking that you will come into my heart, and fill me with your holy spirit that I may learn to live my life for you. I then ask that your love will guide me and teach me to love myself so that I may love others, in Jesus name I pray. If you had prayed this prayer; ask God to make himself known to you. Ask him to sit you under good leadership so that you can hear and learn his word for yourself.**

**And I will give you pastors according to mine heart, which shall feed you with knowledge and understanding. (Jeremiah 3:15)**

God is so rich in mercy, and he forgives us over and over again. It does not matter how many times you will mess up; you can repent and ask God to forgive you. The devil will make accusations against you in your mind, and through others. You will have to cast those thoughts down and speak God's word against him. If God said that your sins are forgiven you than believe him; not the devil

**(Romans 8:35-39) says, "Who shall separate us from the love of Christ? Shall tribulation, or distress, or persecution or famine, or nakedness, or peril, or sword"?**

**As it is written, For thy sake we are killed all the day long; we are accounted as sheep for the slaughter.**

**Nay, in all these things we are more than conquerors through him that loved us.**

**For I am persuaded, that neither death, nor life, nor angels, nor principalities, nor powers, nor things present, nor things to come, nor height, nor depth, nor any other creature, shall be able to separate us from the love of God, which is in Christ Jesus our Lord.**

What I have learned in these few years of theteaching from my heavenly Father is that there is always peace present in true love. When you have a relationship with God, God will reveal to you other people's intentions. He will reveal to you that persons intention, but it is up to you to listen when God forewarn you. He loves you and he will protect you.

I have a greater appreciation for God more than ever before. When I examine my relationship with my children, and see how my children disobey me, and how their disobedience teaches me how God feels about you and I when we disobey him. God wants the best for us just like we want the best for our children. But, we are tying God's hands when we disobey him. We limit what God wants to do in our lives. We are literally breaking God's heart when we do not listen to his instructions.

He loves us so much, that He sent His Word (His only begotten son) to become flesh. Jesus shed His blood, the very thing that connects us to him and God. We are joint heirs with Christ. What God did through Christ made us one with him. He redeemed us; He paid the price on the cross, and restored us back to God. God requires His people to love one another. When you love others the love of God is revealed; Ruth is a very good example.

Ruth and her mother in-law were both stricken with grief from losing their husband by way of death. Naomi wanted Ruth to return to the country she was born out of after the death of their husband, but Ruth refuse to go. She wanted to stay with her mother in-law and she wanted the God of her mother in-law to be her God too. Ruth chose to stay with her mother in-law, and to go wherever she went. When you love and care for others, that love and care is multiplied back to you.

Ruth demonstrated the love of God for her mother in-law Naomi. I learned a lot from Ruth and Naomi's relationship. I learned that when you love and care for another person God will care for you. Your love for others will cause others to take notice. The reason I say this is because when Ruth was gleaning (gathering) in Boaz field. He took notice of her and inquired about her. And he discovered some very important information about her. He knew that she loved and cared for her mother in-law . I believe this is a key characteristic for a man choosing his wife. Because he knows that she will love and care for him. Ladies you yourselves had heard that when a man treats his mom good, he will be good to you too.

**Then said Boaz unto Ruth, Hearest thou not, my daughter? Go not to glean in another field, neither go from hence, but abide here fast by my maidens:**

**Let thine eyes be on the field that they do reap, and go thou after them: have I not charged the young men that they shall not touch thee: and**

**when thou art athirst, go unto the vessels, and drink of that which the young men have drawn.**

**Then she fell on her face, and bowed herself to the ground and said unto him, why have I found grace in thine eyes, that thou shouldest take knowledge of me, seeing I am a stranger?**

**And Boaz answered and said unto her, it hath fully been showed me, all that thou hast done unto thy mother in-law since the death of thine husband; and how thou hast left thy father and thy mother, and art come unto a people which thou knowest not heretofore.**

**The Lord recompense thy work, and a full reward be given thee of the Lord God of Israel, under whose wings thou art come to trust. (Ruth 2:8-12)**

When you trust the Lord, and treat others kindly, you will reap the benefits of kindness being bestowed upon you. Ladies your husband will show up when you learn to care for others more than you care for yourself. I'm not telling you to neglect yourself. What I'm saying to you is to be a caring person; men love a woman who takes care of herself and have a heart to care for others. I'm still learning this myself. I am learning the importance of loving God, and loving others. This is the greatest commandment. When you learn to care for others it's easier to partnership, because there are no chances of selfishness getting in the way.

You could read the rest of the story in its entirety in chapter two of Ruth at your leisure. God has been teaching me and presently teaching me to walk in love and to be a giver. The whole bible is based on love, forgiveness, and giving. I've learned that even faith works by love. If you want the word of God to fall on good ground, you need to keep strife and un-forgiveness out of your relationship.

# CONCEPTION

The word conception defined by Webster is the act of becoming pregnant; the state of being conceived in the womb; the faculty of conceiving in the mind.

God spoke to the prophets of old, using them as a mouthpiece to speak to his people.

God wanted to speak directly to his people, but the people were afraid of God's voice. He allowed them to hear him for themselves, but they refuse to hear God.

**(Exodus 19:9-20), And the Lord said unto Moses, Lo, I come unto thee in a thick cloud, that**

the people may hear when I speak with thee, and believe thee for ever. And Moses told the words of the people unto the Lord.

And the Lord said unto Moses, Go unto the people, and sanctify them today and tomorrow, and let them wash their clothes,

And be ready against the third day: for the third day the Lord will come down in the sight of all the people upon mount Sinai.

And thou shalt set bounds unto the people round about, saying take heed to yourselves, that ye go not up into the mount, or touch the border of it: Whosoever toucheth the mount shall be surely put to death.

There shall not a hand touch it, but he shall surely be stoned, or shot through; whether it be beast or man, it shall not live: When the trumpet soundeth long, they shall come up to the mount.

And Moses went down from the mount unto the people, and sanctified the people; and they washed their clothes.

And he said unto the people, Be ready against the third day: come not at your wives.

And it came to pass on the third day in themorning, that there were thunders and a thick cloud upon the mount, and the voice of the trumpet exceeding loud; so that all the people that was in the camp trembled.

And Moses brought forth the people out of the camp to meet with God; and they stood at the nether part of the mount.

And mount Sinai was altogether on a smoke, because the Lord descended upon it in fire: and the smoke thereof ascended as the smoke of a furnace, and the whole mount quaked greatly.

And when the voice of the trumpet sounded long, and waxed louder and louder, Moses spake, and God answered him by a voice.

(Exodus 20: 18-19), And all the people saw the thunderings, and the lightings, and the noise of the trumpet, and the mountain smoking: and when the people saw it, they removed, and stood afar off.

And they said unto Moses, Speak thou with us, and we will hear: but let not God speak with us, lest we die.

# CONCEPTION

God never said to Moses or the people if they heard him speak they will die, no, he only said not to come up to the mountain, neither touch the mountain. He also said that if he is seen by men they will die; no man has seen God and lived. God set boundaries round about the mountain to keep the people from breaking through.

God had every intention from the beginning to have fellowship and relationship with man. It was Satan who caused the confusion between man and God. He is still doing this this day. He done it to me and he has done it to you too. Somehow we have been thinking that we are not worthy to be spoken to by God. We have wrongly thought that God will not receive us, but he will. God do not look at us as we are, he look at us through the blood of Jesus who sacrifice his life for us. Jesus died that we may live. You will have to use everything that you have in youto resist the accusations of the devil. If you are to conceive, you must have a relationship with God, and spend time in God's word. God's word is your defense.

If you would examine the scene in heaven, the dragon stood before the woman when she was delivering the child; "The child being the word of God". The bible describe the woman travailing and in pain.

Can you imagine this woman persistence in

her pushing in spite of the force against her? "She pushed through the opposing force and delivered the baby (Word)". And the bible said that a war broke out in heaven. (Side bar) "Your break through will cause your enemies to become upset". What caused this war? **"The Word"**. God's word broke fourth and prevailed against Satan's word. I have come to believe that this whole battle between God and Satan is a war over words. God's words always trump Satan's words. The only thing that hinders God's words from performing or manifesting in your life is your unbelief and your confessions. When you speak words that are contrary from what God's word says, you then speak in agreement with the devil. Then God steps back and allow you to have what you say.

**For whosoever shall say unto this mountain, be thou removed, and be thou cast into the sea; and shall not doubt in his heart, but shall believe that those things which he saith shall come to pass; he shall have whatsoever he saith.**

Whenever you hear God's word, receive it, understand it, and meditate on it and keep it you will then become pregnant with his word. Here comes the test, when you hear the word and conceive it, it is your responsibility to protect it. You will have to nurture it, and care for it by feeding yourself the word, and meditating on the word day and night. The seed of

God's word is your baby. How are you going to treat it, and care for it? Jesus explains the parable of the sower to his disciples in (**Matthews 13:18-23).**

**Hear ye therefore the parable of the sower. When any one heareth the word of the kingdom, and understandeth it not, then cometh the wicked one, and catcheth away that which was sown in his heart. This is he which received seed by the way side.**

**But he that received the seed into stony places, the same is he that hears the word, and anon with joy receives it;**

**Yet hath he not root in himself, but endures for a while: for when tribulation or persecution arises because of the word, by and by he is offended.**

**He also that received seed among the thorns is he that heareth the word; and the care of this world, and the deceitfulness of riches, choke the word, and he becometh unfruitful.**

**But he that received seed into the good ground is he that heareth the word, and understandeth it, which also beareth fruit, and bringeth forth, some a hundredfold, some sixty, some thirty.**

Your heart is the ground where the seed of God's

word is sown. When you do not understand it; then comes the wicked one and catches it away. This is exactly what happened to Eve, she didn't understand the word she received from her husband. She said that God told them not to eat from the tree in the midst of the garden, nor to touch it. This is a good example of what happens when you get a word from second hand. God commanded Adam and Adam told Eve his wife. This is beside the point, because Satan still challenged the word spoken to her to cause her to doubt what God had spoken.

We have to take God at his word no matter what. Situations, circumstances, times, people, and seasons will change, but God and his word will remain the same. Take heed to God's spoken word, and learn to take God at his word, especially when he speaks directly to you. Learn to know God's voice, and when he tells you to do something don't allow anyone to turn you away from following through what God have spoken to you.

Take this lesson from the man of God who went to Beth-el to deliver a word from the Lord. The Lord gave him instructions after he had delivered the message, to leave another way and not to stop to eat bread neither drank water in that place.

**And behold, there came a man of God out of Judah by the word of the Lord unto Beth-el: and**

Jeroboam stood by the altar to burn incense.

And he cried against the altar in the word of the Lord, and said, O altar, altar, thus saith the Lord; Behold, a child shall be born unto the house of David, Josiah by name; and upon thee shall he offer the priests of the high places that burn incense upon thee, and men's bones shall be burnt upon thee.

And he gave a sign the same day, saying, This is the sign which the Lord hath spoken; Behold, the altar shall be rent, and the ashes that are upon it shall be poured out.

And it came to pass, when king Jeroboam heard the saying of the man of God, which had cried against the altar in Beth-el that he put forth his hand from the altar, saying, lay hold on him. And his hand, which he put forth against him, dried up, so that he could not pull it in again to him.

The altar also was rent, and the ashes poured out from the altar, according to the sign which the man of God had given by the word of the Lord.

And the king answered and said unto the man of God, entreat now the face of the Lord thy God, and pray for me, that my hand may be restored me again. And the man of God besought the Lord, and the king's hand was restored him again, and became as it was before.

And the king said unto the man of God, Come home with me and refresh thyself, and I will give thee a reward.

And the man of God said unto the king, if thou wilt give me half thine house, I will not go in with thee, neither will I eat bread nor drink water in this place:

For so was it charged me by the word of the Lord, saying, eat no bread, nor drink water, nor turn again by the same way that thou camest.

So he went another way, and returned not by the way that he came to Beth-el.

Now there was an old prophet in Bethel; and his sons came and told him all the works that the man of God had done that day in Beth-el; the words which he had spoken unto the king, them they told also to their father.

And their father said unto them, What way went he? For his sons had seen what way the man of God went, which came from Judah.

And he said unto his sons, saddle me the ass. So they saddled him the ass: and he rode thereon, and went after the man of God, and found him sitting under an oak: and he said unto him, art thou the man of God that camest from Judah?  And he said, I am.

Then he said unto him, come home with me, and eat bread.  And he said, I may not return with thee, nor go in with thee:  neither will I eat bread nor drink water with thee in this place:

For it was said to me by the word of the Lord, thou shalt eat no bread nor drink water there, nor turn again to go by the way that thou camest.  He said unto him, I am a prophet also as thou art; and an angel spake unto me by the word of the Lord, saying, bring him back with thee into thine house, that he may eat bread and drink water.  But he lied unto him.

So he went back with him, and did eat bread in his house, and drank water.  And it came to pass, as they sat at the table, that the word of the Lord came unto the prophet that brought him back:

And he cried unto the man of God that came from Judah, saying, thus saith the Lord, for as much as thou hast disobeyed the mouth of the Lord, and hast not kept the commandment which the Lord thy God commanded thee,

But camest back, and hast eaten bread and drunk water in the place, of the which the Lord did say to thee, eat no bread, and drink no water; thy carcase shall not come unto the sepulcher of thy fathers.

And it came to pass, after he had eaten bread, and after he had eaten bread, and after he had drunk, that he saddled for him the ass, to wit, for the prophet whom he had brought back.

And when he was gone, a lion met him by the way, and slew him: and his carcase was cast in the way, and the ass stood by it, the lion also stood by the carcase. And, behold, men passed by, and saw the carcase cast in the way, and the lion standing by the carcase: and they came and told it in the city where the old prophet dwelt.

And when the prophet that brought him back from the way heard thereof, he said, it is the man of God, who was disobedient unto the word of the Lord: therefore the Lord hath delivered him unto the lion, which hath torn him, and slain him according to the word of the Lord, which he spake unto him.      (1Kings 13:1-26)

When God has spoken directly to you; do not allow anyone to tell you anything different. The devil has no new tricks. He changes the players but the game remains the same. His devises is like an old book with a new cover. The same scheme he used on Eve he now wants to use on you. He wants to challenge the knowledge of God's word you receive. The Bible said when you receive the word the enemy the devil immediately comes to steal it.

When you become pregnant with the word of God; you will need to protect your seed. Let the words from your mouth be in agreement with the word of God. You will have to stand your ground, no matter what. People who are close to you will not understand. You will need to disconnect yourself from some people.

When God sends you a word; it's a word that belongs to you and you alone. You can take a lesson from Mary. When God sent his angel to Mary, listen how Mary responded and the action she took after receiving the word from the Lord.

**(Luke 1:26-38),** and it reads, **And in the sixth month the angel Gabriel was sent from God unto a city of Galilee, named Nazareth, To a virgin espoused to a man whose name was Joseph, of the house of David; and the virgin name was Mary, and the angel came in unto her, and said, Hail, thou that art highly favored, the Lord is with thee: blessed art thou among women.**

**And when she saw him, she was troubled at his saying, and cast in her mind what manner of salutation this should be. And the angel said unto her, fear not, Mary: for thou hast found favor with God.**

**And, behold, thou shalt conceive in thy womb, and bring forth a son, and shalt call his name JESUS. He shall be great, and shall be called the Son of the Highest: and the Lord God shall give unto him the throne of his father David: And he shall reign over the house of Jacob forever; and of his kingdom there shall be no end.**

**Then said Mary unto the, How shall this be, seeing I know not a man? And the angel answered and said unto her, The Holy Ghost shall come upon thee, and the power of the Highest shall over shadow thee: therefore also that holy thing which shall be born of thee shall be called the Son of God.**

I present to you "conception without sexual intercourse". When you become pregnant by God's infallible word, and incorruptible word you will need no human devises. You will never have to worry about a man saying that he's not responsible for your pregnancy. You won't even have to look for the father for child support because God has favored you too. He has given you his word and his word will not return to him void, but it will accomplish into the thing which he sent it.

When you become pregnant you will have to find your connection with somebody that is pregnant too. You see the angel continued to encourage Mary by telling her about her cousin Elisabeth who also conceived according to the word. The angel continued to speak to Mary to give her instructions.

**And, behold, thy cousin Elisabeth, she hath also conceived a son in her old age: and this is the sixth month with her, who was called barren. For with God nothing shall be impossible.**

Mary received God's word from his servant the angel and conceived that very moment.

**And Mary said, Behold the hand maid of the Lord; be it unto me according to thy word. And the angel departed from her.**

After Mary received the word sent from God, Mary immediately connected with someone who touched in agreement with her. Understand this; she didn't get on the phone to boast about her pregnancy. What she did was go to someone who had experienced the same thing that she had experience.

# CONCEPTION

When God had spoken to you; and you hear and understood his word: You become so excited that you can't wait to tell it. But, you are to be very careful with who you will tell it to. It will have to be someone who will celebrate with you, and someone who is pregnant too.

I don't know who that someone could be. But for me, it will have to be someone who is already pregnant and they too can relate to my joy and expectation. The author of Luke continues his story of Mary in **(Luke 1: 39-45),** and it reads, **And Mary arose in those days, and went into the hill country with haste, into a city of Judah;**

**And entered into the house of Zechariah, and saluted Elisabeth. And it came to pass, that, when Elisabeth heard the salutation of Mary, the babe leaped in her womb; and Elisabeth was filled with the Holy Ghost:**

**And she spake out with a loud voice, and said, Blessed art thou among women, and blessed is the fruit of thy womb. And whence is this to me, that the mother of my Lord should come to me?**

**For, lo, as soon as the voice of thy salutation sounded in mine ears, the babe leaped in my womb for joy. And blessed is she that believed: for there shall be a performance of those things which were told her from the Lord.**

Elisabeth rejoiced with Mary. She counted it an honor for Mary to choose her to share her great news. I can attest to how Elisabeth felt, because I have experienced for myself how the Holy Ghost in another person speaking to me had caused my baby (the word) to leap in my womb. **How awesome is the power of agreement?**

Now that you have received the word of God, you will now have to sober and vigilant for the adversary the devil walks about seeking whom he may devour. You will need to be careful what you watch on television, what movies you watch and what and who you listen to.

While you are waiting with great expectation, you may need to separate yourself. You may need to let some people go, and you may need to even separate yourself from the familiar. You will need to go into hiding, until you deliver. You must understand, now that you are carrying something so precious and so valuable, you can expect opposing forces to come against you.

# EXPECTING

You can expect the enemy to come against you in every form and way he can possibly conjure up to attack you. His goal is to get you to denounce the word you received. While you wait for the manifestation of your promise, you should water your seed daily. What I mean when I say water your seed daily is that, you will need to speak to your womb, your inner being with the word of God. You will also need to speak the promises of God in the atmosphere. When you do this you will be putting your angels on an assignment. The angel hearkens to voice of the word of God.

**Bless the Lord, ye his angels that excel in strength, that do his commandments, hearkening unto the voice of his word.   (Psalm 103:20)**

# EXPECTING

You see there is power and life in your spoken words. You will determine what kind of fruit that will grow in your womb, which is your garden. Whatsoever a man sows that is what he will also reap.

This refers to the natural and the spiritual. If you allow yourself to watch or listen to a lot of carnal movies, television shows and radio then you will give birth to a carnal baby. But if you watch, and listen to spiritual programs you will give birth to a holy thing. I have learned over the years that even a pregnant woman in the natural; if she will read to her unborn child in her womb; that child comes out of her womb more alert and smarter than a child who only heard the conversations of the mother's surroundings while in the womb. The conversation the baby hears while in the womb is a little bit of anything and everything; like cussing, fussing, the feeling of oppression, depression you name it. The baby is subject to all that the mother experience while living in her womb.

Every living thing has an ear to hear, and it also speaks. I present to you that the atmosphere we live in is a living thing. "Words have life". When God spoke, he spoke life into everything seen and unseen. We are made in God's image and we too have this same power. Your words have the power of life and death. Jesus said, **"The words that I speak unto you, they are spirit, and they are life".**

**(Proverbs 18:21) says Death and Life is in the power of the tongue. It is with your tongue you can bless or curse.**

Jesus made it obvious how effective our words are, when he spoke to a fig tree and it withered and died. **(Mark 11:12-14)** reads, **And on the morrow, when they were come from Bethany, he was hungry. And seeing a fig tree afar off having leaves, he came, if haply he might find any thing thereon: and when he came to it, he found nothing but leaves; for the time of figs was not yet. And Jesus answered and said unto it, No man eat fruit of thee hereafter for ever. And his disciples heard it.** Please note, that Jesus answered the fig tree. The fig tree spoke to Jesus by having no fruits on its vine.

**(Mark 11:20-21)** reads, **And in the morning, as they passed by, they saw the fig tree dried up from the roots. And Peter calling to remembrance saith unto him, Master, behold, the fig tree which thoucursed is withered away.**

Jesus who is the living Word illustrated to us the power of words and the effect it has on a person or thing. Remember everything is made from a spoken word. You see some of us still do not believe that we give life or death to a thing when we speak. We can literally speak to a thing and it must obey us. You see

God sent his Word and healed us, but you have some people that are walking around still claiming that they are sick. You can have what you say. Then you have some people that want to blame God or question him about why he has not healed them. The answer is under their nose. Healing is made available to you when you receive it.

While you are carrying the seed of the Word, it will be totally up to you what you will deliver. If you want healing, find all the healing scriptures and start speaking them over your body. What you deliver will count on what you will be professing out of your mouth. I will say again, you will have to literally take God at his word. You may not feel like what he hasspoken will come to pass, and it may not look like what he told you will happen. But if God said it, you just keep saying what he said. The angels hearken to the words of God to carry out and to perform the thing that you speak.

**Bless the Lord, ye his angels that excel in strength, that do his commandments, hearkening unto the voice of his word'**

I must warn you, that you must pray and ask God to set a watch before your mouth and to keep the doors of your lips, **"Psalms 141:3"**. You see God can not lie, but your words can cause a breach between you and what God have spoken.  Here now the word of the Lord that was spoken to Moses concerning the children of Israel.

**And the Lord spake unto Moses and unto Aaron saying, how long shall I bear with this evil congregation, which murmur against me?  I have heard the murmurings of the children of Israel, which they murmur against me.**

**Say unto them, as truly as I live, saith the Lord, as ye have spoken in mine ears, so will I do to you: (Numbers 14:26-28)**

God has made us promises and he has not changed his mind.  The words you speak brings to you the very thing you have spoken.  **In v 28, God said, As truly as I live, saith the Lord, as ye have spoken in mine ears, so will I do to you.**  It is your spoken words that will cause the thing to happen.  What are you saying about a thing?

Jesus said it this way in **(Matthew 9:29b), According to your faith be it unto you.  (Matthew 12:36-37) reads, but I say unto you, that every idle word that men shall speak, they shall give account thereof in the day of judgement.  For by thy words thou shalt be justified, and by thy words thou shalt be condemned.  (Mark 11:23) says,  for verily I**

**say unto you, that whosoever shall say unto this mountain be thou removed, and be thou cast into the sea; and shall not doubt in his heart, but shall believe that those things which he saith shall come to pass; he shall have whatsoever he saith.**

Doing your time of expecting you will learn the value of keeping your mouth shut as much as possible. You will learn to speak only when you are speaking in agreement with God's words. Yes, people will take notice, because they will wonder why you aren't saying anything. This is not the time to give any explanation for your quietness. The enemy is after your words. When you speak contrary of the word of God the devil hears it and he will make sure you will get just what you spoken.

You can take a lesson from Zechariah in **(Luke 1:5-20)**, and it reads, **There was in the days of Herod of Judea, a certain priest named Zechariah, of the course of Abijah: and his wife was of the daughters of Aaron, and her name was Elisabeth.**

**And they were both righteous before God, walking in all the commandments and ordinances of the Lord blameless. And they had no child, because that Elisabeth was barren, and they both were now well stricken in years. And it came to pass, that while he executed the priest's office before God in the order of his course.**

According to the custom of the priest's office, his lot was to burn incense when he went into the temple of the Lord. And there appeared unto him an angel of the Lord standing on the right side of the altar of incense.

And when Zechariah saw him, he was troubled, and fear fell upon him. But the angel said unto him, Fear not, Zechariah: for thy prayer is heard; and thy wife Elisabeth shall bear thee a son, and thou shalt call his name John. And thou shalt have joy and gladness; and many shall rejoice at his birth.

For he shall be great in the sight of the Lord, and shall drink neither wine nor strong drink; and he shall be filled with the Holy Ghost, even from his mother's womb. And many of the children of Israel shall he turn to the Lord their God.

And he shall go before him in the spirit and power of Elijah, to turn the hearts of the fathers to the children, and the disobedient to the wisdom of the just; to make ready a people prepared for the Lord.

And Zechariah said unto the angel, whereby shall I know this? For I am an old man, and my wife well stricken in years. And the angel answering said

**unto him, I am Gabriel, that stand in the presence of God; and am sent to speak unto thee, and to show thee these glad tidings.**

**And, behold, thou shalt be dumb, and not able to speak, until the day that these things shall be performed, because thou believeth not my words, which shall be fulfilled in their season.** God had to shut the mouth of Zechariah because he knew that his unbelief and doubt would have hindered the word of God.

**(Ecclesiastes 3:1) says, To everything there is a season, and a time to every purpose under the heaven.**

There is a set time for everything. There is no time in eternity, so when something does not happen at the time that you are expecting it, do not become discouraged.

You will have to understand that this walk you have chosen is a faith walk. It's almost like a game. Have you ever played a game, where there were different obstacle courses you had to go through each one in order to complete the game? In the course of the game, you fought against everything that came against you. Life is like a game; learn to play it well.

# EXPECTING

In real life you also experience different courses and seasons, there are times when you don't know if you will come out a winner or not. But you stay with it, and some how it works out for you. God has made it so that we are winners. He knows what we have to fight with down here that is why he gave us some help.

We have angels that God have given charge over us to keep us in all our ways. The angels hearken to the word of God and every words you speak. The angels carried the words out, but they are performed at the appointed time.

I have learned something about expectation. When you are expecting, the wait seems extremely long sometimes. I have learned that waiting teaches you to be patience, and it also strengthens your faith. Things do not always happen according to plan, so you have to wait some more. I can tell you that waiting can be tempting; you can be tempted to take matters in your own hands. You may be feeling like you should be doing something while you wait.

If you are tempted to do anything; this is what you should do: Start working to prepare for the thing you are expecting. I know from experience, and from giving birth to a natural baby, I went out and brought baby cloths, and baby furniture. All I can tell you is this, from the mouth of Bishop T.D. Jakes **GET READY!**

# GET READY! GET READY!

# GIVING BIRTH

Giving birth will cause you to travail, and the travailing will cause you to experience some pain. The thing that you have been praying about and believing God for is now coming to fruition. You are bringing forth the promise; this is not the time to doubt or to be discouraged. There will be times when you will be tempted to blurt out words that will express your pain; just be careful that you don't curse your baby- by calling it by the pain you experience when you bring it forth. The reason I say this is because when Rachel was giving birth to Benjamin; she was in hard labor and just before her soul was departing from her She called his name Benoni. Benoni means "Son of my Pain". It was Jacob the child's father who spoke and said, "It is not so", the child's name will be called Benjamin, meaning "Son of my right Hand".

**And they journeyed from Beth-el; and there was but a little way to come to Ephrath: and Rachel travailed, and she had hard labor.**

**And it came to pass, when she was in hard labor, that the midwife said unto her, "Fear Not"; thou shalt have this son also.**

**And it came to pass, as her soul was in departing, (for she died) that she called his name Benoni; but his father called him Benjamin.**

So I say to you doing your time of labor and delivery "Be careful" what you say. It is doing this time when you will experience pain and discomfort. I know you may be asking, what is she talking about? I am talking about delivering the Word that is in you. A woman who is naturally pregnant and has carried the baby to full term; the baby will shift into the birth canal. It will position itself to prepare itself for birthing. It is doing this time when the baby is weighing heavy on your uterus, and it causes discomfort. As it is in the natural, so also it is in the spirit. When you are about to deliver what God has promised, you will feel a shifting. There is a shifting that takes place in your attitude, and your environment, when you are about to deliver.

If you have been spending time with God by listening to his word, speaking his word, meditating and reading his word then it is a strong possibility that you are pregnant by the word of God. When you are pregnant with promise, you will know it, because the devil will fight you even harder. Satan will try to frustrate you by causing you to doubt God's word, denounce his word by becoming offended. The devil will try everything he could to oppose God's word, and to get you to denounce the word of God.

When you are physically pregnant you become very emotional. It seems like every little thing would get on your nerves. You start changing your eating habits, watching what you eat and drink.

When you are spiritually pregnant you began to change who you are around, what you listen to, who you listen to, and what you watch on television, and the movies. Your emotions change doing this time too. It is something about hearing the word and reading the word and being around those who are talking about the word. It will cause you to be at peace and full of confidence.

Giving birth to God's promises is going to take physical action. When you are ready to give birth you will have to push. This can and will be painful, but you can do it. God will help you through it. It is doing this time when it feels like God has left you, but your knowing that he will never leave you nor forsake you will give you comfort. You will have to push pass unbelief. This will require you to believe on purpose even when circumstances dictate something to you that is opposite of what you believe. You will have to push pass your haters. Remember that devil hates us. And he will use anyone or anything against us. Push through your past memories, by letting go of those things that remind you of who you were before you received the knowledge of truth. You will have to push yourself to do the word of God. You cannot say you believe God and don't do what he instructs you to do. **Be a doer of the word and not a hearer only.** James says it this way, **Even so faith, if it hath not works, is dead, being alone. (James 2:17)**

Now that you are about to give birth; you will need to make preparation. As I stated before you will need to get ready for your new arrival. I remember some years ago I was listening to Bishop Jakes, and he talked about preparing yourself for the thing that you will be expecting. He said something like this; if you were expecting to meet your husband to be; you will need to fix yourself up and dress like you are going somewhere. Another example came from Steve Harvey who told his radio listener to make a tape or a CD of their music or their live performance, and have it ready; so that when someone ask to see or hear the tape you will have it; with no excuses. He encourage them to do this because he said if someone was to discover them and if they wanted a copy of their music and if they are not prepared then they will miss that opportunity. Another example of preparation is by a man name Roland Martin he stated in an interview by saying, "You never know when opportunity will manifest itself, but you should be prepared for it".

With that being said I now take this time to encourage you to start preparing yourself. And I would say to you that every time you are challenged; you will have to speak what God said concerning your situation. Here is your chance to exercise your faith. You said that you believe God. What will you do when situation appears to be opposite to what you have believed God for? Will you say what you see or will you continue to say what God promise. Listen; believing is a challenge, especially when things look different from what you have been expecting. But a test only comes to make you stronger, especially in faith. Do you know that your faith can be seen? You get nothing from wishing, hoping, and thinking. You will have to do something. Take some lessons from our brothers and sisters in the bible when they were seeking Jesus and expecting to receive.

**And again he (Jesus) entered into Capernaum after some days; and it was noised that he was in the house. And straightway many were gathered together, insomuch that there was no room to**

**receive them, no, not so much as about the door and he preached the word unto them. (Mark 2:1-2)**

**And when they could not come nigh unto him for the press, they uncovered the roof where he was; and when they had broken it up, they let down the bed wherein the sick of the palsy lay. When Jesus saw their faith, he said unto the sick of the palsy, Son, thy sins be forgiven thee. (Mark 2:4-5)**

What I am pointing out here is that faith can be seen. Your words alone when spoken causes the words you speak to begin the work without your physical action. Many times we are face with a situation and the situation appears to be something that will cause us to be at a standstill because we do not know what to do. This is when we have to stand on God's word no matter what. For example; there are so many sick and diseased people among us. We quote all the time **(Isaiah 53:5) He was wounded for our transgression, he was bruised for our iniquities; the chastisement of our peace was upon him; and with his stripes we are healed.** We have quoted this scripture many times; but do we believe it. God's promises were spoken from the beginning of time, and his word is still good today. God has not change, neither has his word. The season and times has change but God remains the same. It is God who changes the season and the times.

**Daniel answered and said, "Blessed be the name of God for ever and ever"; for wisdom and might are his. And he changeth the times and the seasons. (Daniel 2:20-21)**

Your time is in the hand of God. But he gave that time to you in order to see what you will do with it. It's sad to say that many have shortened their time on earth by the words they have spoken. **(Proverbs 18:21)** says, **Death and Life are in the power of the tongue; and they that love it shall eat the fruit thereof.** Our words give life or death. What have you been saying lately? Most of the time when you speak something and because you don't see it after you spoke it does not mean it's not forming. What you don't realize is that when you speak words, words are like seeds. When you plant seeds in the ground you do not see what you planted for a month or longer. You will eventually see something come through the dirt. But not the full plant of what you had in mind. So are your words, when you speak they manifest too.

People do not realize the power of words. I have changed doctors because of the words they spoke to me. I corrected their words after they spoke it, and I know they were offended. But it did not matter to me, because their words will not come to past in my life. You can call me peculiar if you want to because I am. I am a peculiar people because God said that I am. God said that I am a royal priesthood. Jesus said that whatever I bind on earth is bound in heaven. And whatever I loose on earth is loose in heaven. You have to be careful when people talk to you. People will say things to you that you might not want to see happen. But you will have to bind those words in the name of Jesus, and loose the words you desire.

I understand the power of words. There have been lots of self-proclaim prophets rising up over the years. But let me make you understand something: every one of us is a prophet. God made us in his image to be just like him. When God speaks, the thing that he has spoken will happen, and so it is when we speak. The problem is; that when you say something, you forget about it, and you don't realize that what you have spoken had caused that thing to happen because of your spoken words. We are the only creature that God created that can speak language. I say word language just in case there's someone out there saying that animals speak. They do speak. They speak according to the language of that particular animal.

Giving birth can be liberating. Just when you have made all the preparation you could think to do; the devil is standing close by waiting for an opportune time to destroy your seed as soon as you give birth. He may be standing close to devour your baby, but I dare you to be encouraged. Your delivery will give you the victory over the devil. Your seed shall bruise his head. Your seed is your word, and your baby is whatever comes forth through you. You are the only one who knows what you are expecting and believing for.

Giving birth will sometimes cause you to go into hiding. It's not because you are afraid. It's because that devil is seeking to destroy you and your seed. Do you realize how throughout history Satan has been fighting to destroy and to kill our seed (child or children)? Do you remember in the Old Testament how after the promises of God came to fruition concerning the children of Israel? Pharaoh stood against them just like Satan stood against the woman when she was ready to give birth. Let me set the stage for you to understand. Joseph was Israel's (Jacob) favorite son and he was next to the youngest. All of Joseph's brothers were jealous of him except his youngest brother Benjamin. Joseph brothers wanted to kill him after he told him about his dream. **(Side bar)"Be careful who you share your dream with".** But instead they sold him into slavery; and they told their father that an animal had killed him. To make a long story short; God blessed Joseph by giving him favor with Pharaoh, and he was made ruler over all Egypt. A famine took place throughout the land, and Egypt was the only place that had food. Joseph's father and his brothers needed food. Jacobsent his sons into Egypt to purchase food, not knowing that his son Joseph was still alive, and he is the Governor of Egypt.

He was in a position to be a blessing to his family, and his people. The dream Joseph had dream came to past. Joseph reunited with his father and brothers; and they all moved to Egypt. There came a time when Joseph died, and all of his generation. And the Pharaoh who Joseph served under died too.

**And Joseph died, and all his brethren, and all that generation.**

**And the children of Israel were fruitful, and increased abundantly, and multiplied, and waxed exceeding mighty; and the land was filled with them.**

**Now there rose up a new king over Egypt, which knew not Joseph. And he said unto his people, Behold the people of the children of Israel are more and mightier than we: Come on, let us deal wisely with them; lest they multiply, and it come to pass, that, when there falleth out any war, they join also unto our enemies, and fight against us, and so get them up out of the land.**

**Therefore they did set over them taskmasters to afflict them with their burdens. And they built for Pharaoh treasure cities, Pithom and Raamses.**

**But the more they afflicted them, the more they multiplied and grew. ·And they were grieved**

because of the children of Israel. And the Egyptians made the children of Israel to serve with rigor (strictness, and harshness).

And they made their lives bitter with hard bondage, in mortar, and in brick, and in all manner of service in the field: all their service, wherein they made them serve, was with rigor.

And the king of Egypt spake to the midwives, of which the name of the one was Shiprah, and the name of the other Puah.

And he said, when ye do the office of a midwife to the Hebrew women, and see them upon the stool (to give birth); if it be a son, then ye shall kill him: but if it be a daughter, then she shall live.

But the midwives feared God, and did not as the king of Egypt commanded them, but saved the men children alive.

And the king of Egypt called for the midwives, and said unto them, Why have ye done this thing, and have saved the men children alive?

And the midwives said unto Pharaoh, Because the Hebrew women are not as the Egyptian women; for they are lively, and are delivered ere (early) the

**midwives come in unto them.**

**Therefore God dealt well with the midwives: and the people multiplied, and waxed very mighty.**

**And it came to pass, because the midwives feared God, that he made them houses.**

**And Pharaoh charged all his people, saying, Every son that is born ye shall cast into the river, and every daughter ye shall save alive. (Exodus 1:6-22)**

Your birthing process will prompt you to become stronger, and you will muster up strength that you didn't even know you had. I have told you before, that when you are pregnant and when you are about to deliver; you will have to go into hiding. When you are celebrating your happiness, everyone is not happy for you. You see, you cannot allow the enemy to know everything. Remember he is after your seed. Do you remember when Mary was pregnant with Jesus, and the angel of the Lord came to Joseph in a dream?

**Now the birth of Jesus Christ was on this wise: when as his mother Mary was espoused (engaged or to take in marriage) to Joseph, before they came together, she was found with child of the Holy Ghost.**

**Then Joseph her husband, being a just and not willing to make a public example, was minded to put her away privily.**

**But while he thought on these things, behold, the angel of the Lord appeared unto him in a dream, saying, Joseph, thou son of David, fear not to take unto thee Mary thy wife; for that which is conceived in her is of the Holy Ghost.**

**And she shall bring forth a son, and thou shalt call his name JESUS: for he shall save his people from their sins.   (Matthew 1:18-21)**

Joseph was an obedient servant of God.   The bible describes him as being just.   He had to have a relationship with God, and a spiritual ear to hear him. When you are pregnant, you will have to listen for instructions, and direction.   You will need the guidance of the Holy Spirit.   Your relationship with God is going to make all the difference doing your birthing process. You do know that the devil is alive here on earth waiting for every opportunity to persecute us women and our seeds (children).

When Jesus was born doing the time that Herod was king; there were wise men who asked of Jesus where about because they wanted to worship him. When King Herod heard this he was troubled.   He then lied to the wise men about wanting to worship Jesus too. He told them to let him know as soon as they find him, because he wanted to worship him too. "That devil is a liar". The king only wanted to know where Jesus was because he wanted to kill him. After the wise men never returned to the king; the king became angry and he ordered all the children under the age of two to be killed. He was searching out to kill Jesus.

**Then Herod, when he saw that he was mocked of the wise men, was exceeding wroth, and sent forth, and slew all the children that were in Beth-le-hem, and in all the coast thereof, from two years old and under, according to the time which he had diligently inquired of the wise men. (Matthew 2:16)**

You have to remember that Jesus was born after forty-two generation since the promise was first given. God had to first put things in order, in order to send Jesus at the appointed time; he had to prepare the people for his coming. All throughout scripture God used the worldly priest and prophets to do rituals in performing sin offerings with goats, lambs, doves, and bullocks. The animal's blood was used to make atonement for the sins of the people. The priest performed these ceremonies yearly for the offering of the people sins. But these offerings never satisfied God, it was only a substitute for what would be to come.

The day of promise has now come when Jesus was born; and he manifested the God fulfilled promise that was spoken of through the prophets that a child will be born through a virgin.

**Therefore the Lord himself shall give you a sign; Behold a virgin shall conceive, and bear a son, and shall call his name Immanuel. (Isaiah 7:14)**

**For unto us a child is born, unto us a son is given; and the government shall be upon his shoulder; and his name shall be called Wonderful, Counselor, The mighty God, The everlasting Father, The Prince of Peace. (Isaiah 9:6)**

Jesus is the Lamb of God, sent by God to be born through a womb of a woman; to be a living sacrifice for the sins of this whole world. God sent him in human flesh to live among us to show us the way to God. He showed us how to pray, how to separate oneself from the world, and to put God first. He taught us to walk in power and authority as sons and daughters of God. Jesus was fully God and he was fully man. He experienced temptation the same as we experience temptation. God sent his son (word) that looks just like us in order that we may relate to him. He wasn't accepted by the people. He was rejected. You have to remember that the people doing those days had a mind-set to worship objects, and they made things and people their idols. That's why you have to be careful what you worship, and who you put before God.

The prophets spoke about Jesus the Messiah coming. The people didn't think he would come out of the under privilege city of Nazareth. This is how some people will judge you, when they see you coming. They will think because you came from the projects, or from a foreign country you are not a candidate to be used by God. Well I got news for you; "We are all candidates to be used" no matter what walk of life we come from. We are justified by grace through faith of Jesus Christ. God used Jesus to break down every barrier that stood against us.

**But now in Christ Jesus ye who sometimes were far off are made nigh by the blood of Christ.**

**For he is our peace, who hath made both one, and hath broken down the middle wall of partition between us;**

**Having abolished in his flesh the enmity, even the law of commandments contained in ordinances; for to make in himself of twain one new man, so making peace;**

**And that he might reconcile both unto God in one body by the cross, having slain the enmity thereby: (Ephesians 2:13-16)**

Because Jesus sacrificed his life and shed his blood for us, God forgave us of all of our sins. He was the propitiation (Jesus shed blood as an offering to God turned away the wrath of God and his shed blood was an atonement that reconciled us back to God). Remember when sin entered the earth through disobedient, sin caused us to be separated from God, and it was the shedding of blood through the crucifixion of Jesus that united us back to God.

**Being justified freely by his (God's) grace through the redemption that is in Christ Jesus.**

**Whom God hath set forth to be a propitiation through faith in his (Jesus) blood, to declare his (Jesus) righteousness for the remission of sins that are past, through the forbearance of God. (Romans 3:24-25)**

**He is despised and rejected of men, a man of sorrows, and acquainted with grief; and we hid as it were our faces from him; he was despised, and we esteemed him not.**

**Surely he hath borne our griefs, and carried our sorrows; yet we did esteem him stricken, smitten of God, and afflicted.**

**But he was wounded for our transgression, he**

**was bruised for our iniquities; the chastisement of our peace was upon him; and with his stripes we are healed.**

**All we like sheep gone astray; we have turned everyone to his own way; and the Lord hath laid on him the iniquity of us all.**

**He was oppressed, and he was afflicted, yet he opened not his mouth; he is brought as a lamb to the slaughter, and as a sheep before her shearers is dumb, so he openeth not his mouth. (Isaiah 53:3-7)**

God has provided us with everything we would need that pertains to life and godliness. We do not have to search outwardly for it because it is inside of us. I know that I had spoken a lot about God's word and his promise, but his word is made available to all of us who believe.

It will be entirely up to you. There are gifts lying on the inside of you. Don't allow the enemy of fear, doubt, and unbelief to hinder your gifts. God has promise to bless you and your seeds (children). You just have to take God at his word. Jesus has already finished the work that was to be done here on earth. There is nothing else to be done. Because of what Jesus done for you, and this whole world, you are now the righteousness of God.

## GIVING BIRTH

Knowing the revelation of Jesus Christ and his finished work is enough to equip, and empower all believers to walk in victory. The bible tells us that we can overcome the enemy (Satan, demons, witches, etc.) by the blood of the Lamb (Jesus) and the word of our testimony.

**And the great dragon was cast out, that old serpent, called the Devil, and Satan, which deceiveth the whole world; he was cast out into the earth, and his angels were cast out with him.**

**And I heard a loud voice saying in heaven, now is come salvation, and strength, and the kingdom of our God, and power of his Christ; for the accuser of our brethren is cast down, which accused them before our god day and night.**

**And they overcame him by the blood of the Lamb, and by the word of their testimony; and they loved not their lives unto the death. (Revelation 12:9-11)**

You can boldly plead the blood of Jesus over yourself, your children, your home, your finances, your job, and even against your enemies. "You plead the blood of Jesus". The bible is very clear when it says that salvation, strength, the kingdom of God, and the power of his Christ has already been established since the foundation of the world.

# WALKING IN VICTORY

Because of the blood of Jesus, we can serve God without fear of our enemies.

You can walk in total victory when you know and understand that God has provided the sacrifice for our sins. God made the provision for our sins in heaven. He has put his word inside of us; with the expectation for us to live victoriously as he had planned for our lives. Jesus was the manifested word sent from God. His word lives on the inside of us. This is the mystery spoken of by Paul, when he said that Christ is in us the hope of glory. God has given us his word and he is not giving us anything else.

God has given us his word, and we in return

ought to believe what he had spoken and expect his word to manifest in our lives.

You can live in total victory by believing, knowing and understanding the finished work of Jesus Christ when he died on the cross, rouse from the dead, went to hell so that you won't go there, defeated Satan and his kingdom, took back all power and authority that was lost in the garden, and now sits on the right hand of God making intercession for us.

**For as much then as the children are partakers of flesh and blood, he also himself like wise took part of the same, that through death he might destroy him that had the power of death, that is, the devil;**

**And deliver them who through fear of death were all their lifetime subject to bondage. (Hebrews 2:14-15)**

Death has no power over us. Jesus is the resurrection. Before Jesus tasted the death for us, the saints that died were in their graves with no chance of ever having life again. The Bible says that the veil of the temple was torn from the top to the bottom. Jesus death and resurrection removed barriers, and allowed us access to our Father God.

**Jesus when he had cried again with a loud voice; yielded up the Ghost (Spirit). And, behold,**

**the veil of the temple was rent in twain from the top to the bottom; and the earth did quake, and the rocks rent;**

**And the graves were opened; and many bodies of the saints which slept arouse, and came out of the graves after his resurrection, and went into the holy city, and appeared to many. (Matthew 27:50-53)**

You don't have to be afraid of dying, because Jesus had taken the sting out of death. He has given us hope for tomorrow. When we die, we are not eternally dead. Jesus has defeated Satan once and for all. We ought to live like we have the victory.

**So when this corruptible shall have put on incorruptible, and this mortal shall have put on immortality, then shall be brought to pass the saying that is written, Death is swallowed up in victory.**

**O death, where is thy sting? O grave, where is thy victory?**

**The sting of death is sin; and the strength of sin is the law.**

**But thanks be to God, which giveth us the victory through our Lord Jesus Christ. (1 Corinthians 15:54-57)**

Satan has nothing over us. He is beneath us. The only thing that will cause you to be defeated by the devil and his demons is your unbelief, and your failure to trust God.

When you are challenged, this is your opportunity to exercise your faith. Faith is believing something even when you don't see no way possible for something to happen. The bible describes what faith is, but it will mean absolutely nothing if you don't apply the word to your life.

**Now faith is the substance of things hoped for, the evidence of things not seen. (Hebrews 11:1)**

The word faith has been defined in many different ways, when described by preachers/ teachers of the word. I personally didn't grasp the concept of it until I got tired of not seeing the results of what I hoped for. I can only explain to you how faith works according to my own personal experience. I hope you understand that God has given us all a measure of faith, so we all have it. If you remember even the disciples asked Jesus to increase their faith. Jesus responded to them by saying,

**If you had faith as a grain of mustard seed, you might say unto this sycamine tree, Be thou plucked up by the root, and be thou planted in the sea; and it should obey you. (Luke 17:6)**

Your faith is only as strong as your confession. Your circumstances and your situation should not dictate what you say or think. Situations and circumstances are always temporary. You will have to learn to speak what you believe and not what you feel. Here lies the key to strengthening your faith; Stop saying what you see. Say what you are expecting to see. I know this sound foreign to you right now, but faith is believing God, and believing what you hope for even when you can't or even when you don't see it. All throughout the Bible men and women were faced with all kinds of challenges, and all they sometimes had was a word from the prophet of God and sometimes false prophets that offered them hope.

The Bible is the only living truth that will give you life. You will not find it in no other book. You will not find life in using drugs, nor drinking alcohol, you will not find it in a clothing line, nor will you find it in the promises made by man. You will only find what you are looking for in Jesus Christ. He has what you are looking for. God has set before you death and life, blessings and curses, he said choose life so that you and your seed may live.

The Bible is not as complicated as man try to make it to be. God sent his son Jesus, and Jesus sent us the Holy Spirit to be a comforter to us, and to be a helper to us. The Holy Spirit will lead and guide you unto all truth. Jesus said that he is the way, the truth, and the life, and no man can come to the Father (God), but by him (Jesus).

Don't be deceived by the glamour of this world. When Jesus was here on earth the devil tempted Jesus by offering him the kingdom of this world if he would bow down and serve him. You don't want to make any deals with the devil. He don't own nothing. God owns everything, and he gave it to us. The earth belongs to us, God told us to replenish it, be fruitful and multiply, and to have dominion over every creeping thing, and over the birds of the air, and every fish of the sea. You don't even want to accept anything from devil. He is a liar, a thief, a deceiver, a murderer, and an impersonator. The bible says that he disguises himself as an angel of light. You will need the Holy Ghost to help you discern that lying spirit.

If you are going to be equipped with faith, you will have to take the bible and arm yourself with the truth that is inside of it. You have to read it, meditate on it every day. It will make you stronger in faith. The Word of God is in you, but you need another witness. The bible says that out of the mouths of two or three witnesses the word is establish. When you speak God's word you are agreeing with God, Jesus and the Holy Spirit.

You can live a victorious life when you are armed with the word of God. The word of God is in you. God has planned it that way. The woman in the book of Revelation is all of us who believe. We are the church, and we are the bride of Christ. He is coming back for us. But until he do we have to live the abundant life he promised we can have here on earth. We can live victoriously, and we can operate in the same power Jesus demonstrated when he was here on earth. How? It will be according to your belief. Jesus is not dead. He is alive in me, and he is alive in you. Your words are spirits, it gives life or death. Jesus is the word. If you want to walk in victory speak the word. The word of God you speak will deliver you and your children. You will have to open your mouth and give voice to God's word, so that his word will give life.

**It is not in heaven, that thou (you) shouldest say, who shall go up for us to heaven, and bring it unto us. That we may hear it, and do it?**

**Neither is it beyond the sea, that thou (you) shouldest say, who shall go over the sea for us, and bring it unto us, that we may hear it, and do it?**

**But the word is very nigh (near) thee (you), in thy (your) mouth, and in thy (your) heart, that thou (you) mayest do it. (Deuteronomy 30:12-14)**

**But the righteousness which is of faith speaketh on this wise, Say not in thine (your) heart, Who shall ascend into heaven? (that is, to bring Christ down from above:)**

**Or, who shall descend into the deep? (that is to bring up Christ again from the dead.)**

**But what saith it? The Word is nigh (near) thee (you), even in thy (your) mouth, and in thy (your) heart; that is, the Word of faith, which we preach; (Romans 10:6-8)**

The Word of God should be in your heart and in your mouth. You don't have to tarry for it, you don't have to wait to get to heaven to receive it, but the Word is near you. You will overcome, and you will defeat the enemy with the words you speak out of your own mouth. The enemy comes for the word. When you have heard the word and understood the word, the enemy will come to get you to start doubting what you heard and what too believe. Stand strong in your belief. When you learn to take God at his word you will then enter into his rest.

**Let us therefore fear (believe), lest, a promise being left us of entering into his rest, any of you should seem to come short of it.**

**For unto us was the gospel preached, as well as unto them:  but the word preached did not profit them, not being mixed with faith in them that heard it.**

**For we which have believed do enter into rest, as he said, As I have sworn in my wrath, if they shall enter into my rest: although the works were finished from the foundation of the world. (Hebrews 4:1-3)**

When we believe God and doubt not, we too as believers will enter into his rest.  If you read on in Hebrews, you will read that some entered not into his rest because of unbelief.  There are times when believers attend to faint, and get weary in there walk because they do not see what God has promise them come to life doing their life time.  I beseech you to hold fast to your belief, it will happen.  If God promised it, it will happen just like he said.  Faith is believing even when you do not see it.  Faith is taking God at his word.

God has given you his Word.  Now it is up to you to possess it.  His Word belongs to you.  The Holy Spirit gave me a revelation of the promise land.  God promised a land to the children of Israel.  This land is flowing with milk and honey.  The land is Canaan; this land belongs to us; it was promised to our forefathers.  God delivered the children of Israel out of Egypt.  But when he delivered them their mind was still in bondage to the land where he brought them from. They journeyed in the wilderness for forty years. They complained, and murmured the whole time. God provided for them, he showed them great and mighty acts, but they still did not believe. I am saying this to say this; why aren't we trying to get to this rich place of promise? Here is the revelation, the promise land is not a place; it's a state of mind. God was testing them to reveal what was in their heart. I am asking you today, while you are on your journey, what else is there to prove? The scripture in Romans is very clear; if we are to be transformed we will have to renew our minds.

**I beseech you therefore, brethren, by the mercies of God, that ye present your bodies a living sacrifice, holy, acceptable unto God, which is your reasonable service.**

**And be not conformed to this world: but be ye transformed by the renewing of your mind, that ye may prove what is that good, and acceptable, and perfect, will of God.    (Romans 12:1,2)**

If you are going to receive all that God has given to you, you will need to start with a change of mind. When you see pastors, and other saved brothers and sisters walking in victory, it is because they have taken hold of God's promises and they are running with it.

The word of God is not just for pastors. His word is for believers. Do you believe God? If you believe him, you should not be waiting on him. He has given you everything, even his only begotten son. Now what are you going to do with what he has given you?

Let me help you some more. Jesus has given us the keys to unlock heaven and earth. He said that whatever we bind on earth is bound in heaven and whatever we loose on earth is loose in heaven. The words from your mouth are the key. You have the authority. I don't know what can be preventing you to walk in victory, but if it is your past, you need to let it go right now.

**Brethren, I count not myself to have apprehended: but this one thing I do, forgetting those things which are behind, and reaching forth unto those things which are before,**

**I press toward the mark for the prize of the high calling of God in Christ Jesus. (Philippians 3:13,14)**

Letting go is not easy, but if you will let that thing go, and press forward you will be able to receive something new. God can't give you something new if you are holding on to the old thing. I use want to understand the scripture about the new wine being poured into old wine skins, and the new cloth placed on the old garment; I wanted to know what that meant, and I asked God. Don't you know he revealed it to me? I wanted to change, but I couldn't change because I was still holding on to the past. The scripture I am referring to is found in two places of the Bible; you can find it in Matthews, and Mark.

**No man also seweth a piece of new cloth on an old garment, else the new piece that filled it up taketh away from the old , and the rent is made worse.**

**And no man putteth new wine into old bottles: else the new wine doth burst the bottles, and the wine is spilled, and the bottles will be marred: but new wine must be put into new bottles. (Mark 2: 21,22)**

How can God pour new revelation, new information, new things, and new people in your life when your mental capacity is stuck in an old place? If God was to pour something in you it will leak out. You will not be able to retain it. When God began to reveal this truth to me, he began sending me word in relation to renewing my mind. God fed me word of truth to counter block the lies that were built up in my wrong thinking.

I want you to say this statement out loud to yourself; **If it is to be it is up to me.** No one can do this but you. This journey is a faith walk. I can believe with you, and for you, but when you believe for yourself you become a threat to your enemies. God has done something for you, and there is no denying it. You will overcome the enemy by the words of your testimony, and by the Blood of the Lamb.

# CLOSING REMARKS

I am finish. I hope your faith is strengthening. I tried my best to share with you what God has placed in my spirit. I wanted to make you aware of why the enemy (the devil) fights us women like he does. It's because he is angry with us. He hates us. He is angrier with us women more than he is with the men. He is the one who is behind every pain, every hurt, and every sorrow you will ever experience. I personally believe that he is behind using our men against us and using them against themselves. I believe that Satan is the cause of our men turning away from being in our lives and in the lives of our sons and daughters. The reason I say this is because the Men are the priest of the house. They were created as headship. The enemy has done a job on causing division between a male and female relationship. He has accomplished hurting us by hurting our men, and our sons.

Listen up women, we need to stop fighting one another, and start fighting our real enemy. Our real enemy is the devil, his demons, principalities, powers, and spiritual wickedness in higher places. The devil has used us against each other. The Lord spoke to me about speaking to women some years ago, and he led me to this scripture.

Thus saith the Lord of host, consider ye, and call for the mourning women, that they may come; and send for cunning (skill employed in a crafty manner) women, that they may come:

And let them make haste and take up a wailing for us, that our eyes may run down with tears, and our eyelids gush out with waters. (Jeremiah 9:1,18)

Yet hear the word of the Lord, O ye women, and let your ear receive the word of his mouth, and teach your daughters wailing, and everyone her neighbor lamentation.

For death is come up into our windows, and is entered into our palaces, to cut off the children from without, and the young men from the streets.

Speak, Thus saith the Lord even the carcases of men shall fall as dung upon the open field, and as the handful after the harvestman, and none shall gather them. (Jeremiah 9:20-22)

This scripture relates to the many deaths of the men doing that time. The commentator interprets these verses as the number of men will be insufficient; so severe and widespread will be the death scene, that the female population at large will be needed in order that lamentations may be made for all the dead.

I believe we as women are so powerful. I believe

the reason why there are so many of us gathered in churches is because we are the weeping women the bible verse spoke about. We are lamenting for our husbands, sons, and love ones. Jesus has always been sensitive to our emotions. I believe Jesus was closest to us because we are his bride. There is something significant about us, and the reason some men don't see us as the bride we are is because the enemy is using the men against us to hurt us. But I dare you to receive the love of God to your hurt, and your wounded heart. God's love is greater than a temporary feeling. God loves you. He will take care of you better than any man can. Don't allow yourself to mourn over the loss of a relationship. I'm not saying not to have relationship, but don't allow the relationship to have you all wrapped up that you forget about God.

I believe the reason Jesus had a heart of compassion more so for women, is because he knew that the devil would fight us the most. When you read the bible and you read about the women following Jesus, and ministering to Jesus; and then how the men would look with indignation when Jesus would take the time to speak with them. You will see how Jesus always defended them.

I want to use this time to express my heart to all who will read this book. I'm not sure if I was clear in expressing what I wanted you to understand. If not, I hope that this scripture in Revelation will prompt you to study the book of revelation. There is so much meat in this particular book. I will need more time to really write more, but I hope you seek God and the Holy Spirit to help you understand God's word. From the time I have been writing this book there has been so many different distractions that came up against my writing.. I am not giving up on writing and I am completing what I had started.

Ladies; You have the anointed one living on the inside of you, and so do you men. But there is something about us women that causes us to be a threat to Satan and his kingdom.

I am speaking from my heart when I say this; please live your life as if you know that your God is the Almighty, All Powerful, and He has made us to have dominion over our enemies. Jesus restored (reconciled) us back to God. **Do not live a defeated life.** You are chosen of the Lord. You are the apple of his eye.

If you have never been in love before; fall in love with our maker. He loves you with an everlasting Love. It is okay to love a man, but that man is flesh, and he's imperfect. Learn to love God and he will teach you how to love; and he will teach you how to be loved. Man will make you feel good for a moment, but God will make you feel good forever.

God is the best security you could ever have. When you learn what God says in his word concerning you, you will never be afraid another day in your life.

If you are condemning yourself stop it right now.  God is greater than your condemnation.

**For if our heart condemn us, God is greater than our heart, and knoweth all things.**

**Beloved, if our heart condemn us not, then have we confidence toward God.  (1 John 3:20,21)**

I pray that you are receiving this.  I use to walk around feeling condemn all the time. And I am talking about the majority of the time I was save.  I wasn't walking in the victory where with Christ had made me free.  It wasn't until I heard the teaching of Creflo Dollar speaking on "The righteousness of God" at one of his Minister's and Leadership Conference at World Changers Church in College Park Georgia 2001.  He made the word very clear.  I no longer had to believe the lies of the devil.  That devil kept reminding me of what I did in the past, by bringing up things that happen to me in my childhood.  I felt ashamed and I felt condemned.  When you don't understand all that Jesus did for you when he died on the cross, you are subject to live defeated. The accusation comes from the devil, and it is the trick of the enemy. He is our accuser. He will bombard your thoughts, and your mind with accusation.  Don't believe him or your feelings.  Your thoughts have a way of making you feel a certain way because of the wrong thoughts you think.  I know this because it happened to me. "Stop beating yourself up".  You are beautiful.  You are fearfully and wonderfully made. You have to believe what God says about you. If you would just read God's word, and take God at his word, you will come to know that God is true to his word. When you read and study God's word you will discover that everything that was needed to satisfy God was fulfilled through the shed blood of Jesus Christ.

**For the promise that he should be the heir of the world, was not to Abraham, or to his seed, through the law, but through the righteousness of faith. (Romans 4:13)**

In closing; it is entirely up to you to bring forth the promises of God which he has spoken. His promises belong to you. You are pregnant with promise. The word of God is in you. You bring forth his promises when you speak what God has said, and watch his word do the work. His word will perform when it is spoken and believed. The word of God is in you and it lives. It cannot die. God's word is pregnant, and he has put his word inside of you. Why don't you give birth to it, by speaking it, meditating on it, believing it, and living it? If you don't live your life to the fullest now, you will never get that chance. It has been appointed once for a man to live and once for a man to die. There are two dates given to us, our birth date and our death date. There is a dash in between that tells others what you have done with your life. I read a book entitled "Robbing the Grave of its Greatness" by Delatorro L. McNeal the second. And I would like to share a quote from one of the pages.

It says "Don't Let it die in you! My friend, when this dash of life is over, everything that you did not give birth to, with some form of documentation or communication of the dream or vision, will die with you. When you die, it dies! When you die, that business idea dies! When you die, that book idea dies! When you die that song lyric dies! When you live your life, make sure that you are continually giving birth to something. Why? Because if you are continually giving birth to something, even when you die, IT STILL LIVES! Become a license grave robber, as a result, when you die, it lives on! When you die, that business idea lives in your family! When you die, that song is sung and heard around the world! When you die, that dream was birthed and given life! Sometimes our dreams will come true within our lifetime, but as long as the dream and the vision are PUT OUT THERE, then we all have something to live up to.** He stated that Goodness is free, but Greatness will cost you". This quote is from the book "Robbing the grave of its greatness" by Delatorro McNeal. You can purchase his book at Amazon.com. This quote from his book caused my baby to leap in my wound, how about you?

# GIVING HONOR

I would like to give honor to some very special people in my life. I first want to give honor to God, who kept me through many hard and tough times. I honor God for making me his choice among the chosen. I honor God for allowing me to live beyond the Doctor's report and all the haters. I honor God for making known to me who I am in him, and who he is. He is God, and there is no other. I honor you God, your Word, and your Holy Spirit. Thank You, Thank You, Thank You.

I want to acknowledge, and honor my son Jeffery Blackwell. I want to honor him by sharing a small portion of his gift with all of you who read this book. He wrote this poem for my oldest deceased son Gregory doing the time of his death. My son Jeff has many talents, and I am exposing one of them right now. I love you son.

# IT'S A SHAME

It's a Shame.  I can say it now instead of saying it
before.
I wish I would've said I love you!
I wish we would've said more!
I know God has the key to all understanding, even
things we can't understand.
I don't understand why you're gone so soon, but I
know God has a better plan;
No more tears!  No more grief!  You are never too far.
I know that the pain is here on earth and peace is
where you are.
When I think of you I think of Christ for I know
through him you have eternal life.
You will always be remembered.
We will always miss you.
You will live on in our hearts forever and We WILL
NEVER FORGET YOU.

*BY:  JEFFERY K. BLACKWELL*

I want to acknowledge, and honor my daughter Noelle Blackwell for her creativity and her business smarts. She is planning to open her own business someday. I honor her while I am still here. I love you.

I want to acknowledge, and honor my son Anthony Blackwell Jr. for his creative art skills. He has drawing skills that will someday be seen by millions. I honor you today. I love you.

I want to acknowledge, and honor my deceased nephew Michael Angelo Lanham who went home to be with the Lord, and died with a drawing gift inside of him. He wanted to make comic books. But his drawings never made it to the public eye. In memory of his gift I do honor him.

I want to acknowledge, and honor my oldest deceased brother Edward Rawls who died with his gifts inside of him. My brother had a love for writing songs. But, he never copy written any of them, nor did he have anyone to sing them. I honor his gift.

I am proud to honor and to acknowledge my sister Hattie Wilson and her fiancé Harvis Satcher for putting together a copy-written prayer and a song. Below is a copy of their prayer. The CD of the song has not yet been released.

# THE BLOOD OF JESUS NEVER LOST ITS POWER

Everlasting Father: The creator of heaven and all therein. Father we come through your son Jesus, to give thanks to you for your goodness, for your mercy, for your grace, we thank you for who you are. You is the almighty God. Hallelujah to God the Father, to God the son, to the Holy Spirit; Thank you Jesus for what you did, for mankind, you made a way by shedding your blood, and you layed your life down on the cross., for the remission of sin. And the third day you arose with all Power and Authority in your hands. Thank you Jesus for doing God's will. Thank you Father for sending your son, Thank you Holy Spirit for your guidance, Father let your let your kingdom come, and let your will be done, on earth as it is in heaven.

Father God we come as Christians with short coming; we have sinned, forgive us Lord for all the sin, that we have committed, forgive us for every evil thought, continue to provide us with wisdom and knowledge of your Word; so that we may become a better Christian.

And yes we claim the blood of Jesus over our health; for the blood never lost its power. The blood prevails over our adversary; over our finance. We claim the blood over our children, over our grandchildren, over our great grandchildren; the blood prevails over our mothers and our fathers, over our sisters and brothers, over our sister in laws and over our brother in laws, over our nieces and nephews, and yes we claim the blood over America; God Bless America, heal our land.

Father God we claim the benefits you provide for us in **(Isaiah 54:17)**, No weapon that is formed against thee shall prosper and every tongue that rise against thee in judgment thou shalt condemn. This is the heritage of the servants of the Lord, and their righteousness is of me, saith the Lord.

By: Hattie Wilson and Harvis Satcher

I want to acknowledge my Mom Hilda Meredith who is 85 years old by the time this book is printed. She is still alive and doing well. I want to honor my mom for her long suffering of love she endured, and bestowed upon us. I honor my Mom for sacrificing her life to give us a life. I honor this strong woman who endured the test of times. I honor her life today. I love you mom.

I want to acknowledge, and honor all of my grandchildren, my nieces, nephews, brothers and sisters who are pregnant with Greatness. I say to all of you, "Let your gifts be made known": leave a mark in the earth. God has given all of us a gift, and a talent, "Do not be like the man with the one talent in the bible who hid his talent in the earth. God is looking for some fruit. I love y'all

I want to acknowledge Breana Fisher who was not afraid to use her gift of drawing. I honor her, and I acknowledge her gift. She is the artist who courageously drew my front cover of this book. She is presently in high school and she loves to draw. If you need a design created you can contact her via e-mail. Her e-mail address is found in the front of the book. Thank You so much Breana

I want to acknowledge and honor my daughter's godmother Denise Westray and her husband Rudy Westray. Thank you for your unselfish love, and your willingness to always give a helping hand. Thank you for assisting me in raising my daughter. Thank you for your long suffering while enduring her teenage years. Thank You for your prayers. I love you both.

I want to give a special thanks to everyone who purchases this book and those who will read this book. It may not be the best book you ever read, but I sure appreciate your support. Thank You for allowing me to share my gift with you and to the world.

# AUTOBIOGRAPHY

Gloria Ann Blackwell was born Gloria Ann Meredith to Hilda Mae, and Benjamin Larry Meredith. She is a mother of four adult children, Gregory who is deceased, Jeffery, Anthony, and Noelle Blackwell, and the grandmother of twelve grandchildren. She is a Graduate of Greater Mt. Calvary Bible Institute, where she received a certificate in Biblical Studies in 2003, and certification in ministry in 2003. She was ordained and license by Archbishop Alfred A. Owens Jr. of Greater Mt. Calvary Holy Church in Washington D, C. She accepted Jesus Christ as her personal savior, and was baptized at the age of eleven. Her love for God grew stronger as she grew in age. God confirmed his calling for her through a dream in the year of 2001; he awakened her from her sleep with Isaiah 43. She humbly acknowledges that she is only God's witness the one he has chosen. She is the future CEO and founder of "Living Your Dream Network" a non-profit organization. This organization will work to empower, inform and to provide the tools necessary to help others live their dream.

# WALKING IN VICTORY

We can live and walk in total victory because Jesus Christ won the battle against Satan, all his demons, and the principalities and powers.